Hidden Manna:

A Dream Journey to Enlightenment

Hidden Manna:

A Dream Journey to Enlightenment

Chris Doolin and Daya Devi-Doolin

Padaran Publications
Deltona, FL 32725
USA

Hidden Manna: A Dream Journey to Enlightenment, Copyright © 2022, Chris Doolin and Daya Devi-Doolin, Padaran Publications, Deltona, FL 32725.

All Rights Reserved, including the right to reproduce the book, or any portion thereof, in any form without prior permission of the Publisher, except for the inclusion of brief quotations in a review.

Publisher's Note

The Publisher and Authors shall have neither liability nor responsibility to any person or organization with respect to any loss or damage caused or alleged to be caused directly or indirectly by the information contained in this book. The purpose of this book is to educate, entertain and stimulate. This book is sold with the understanding that the Publisher and Authors are not involved in offering legal, medical or psychological service.

ISBN: 978-1-877945-27-4
2nd Edition

Sales: http://www.padaran.com   Email: padaran@padaran.com
Telephone: +1 (386) 532-5308
Book Cover Graphic Designer:
Chris Doolin

Printed in the United States of America
Padaran Publications
1794 N. Acadian Dr. Deltona, FL 32725

Other Books by Daya Devi-Doolin

Super Vita-Minds: How to Stop Saying I Hate You…To Yourself!
Americans Saving Ourselves Together
The Only Way Out Is In: The Secrets of the 14 Realms to Love, Happiness and Success
Yoga, Meditation and Spirituality for African American Community: If You Can Breathe, You CAN Do Yoga
Grow Thin While You Sleep
I AM POWER: Divine Affirmations
Dabney's Handbook on A Course in Miracles

Other Books by Chris Doolin and Daya Devi-Doolin

Smile America

Children's books by Daya Devi-Doolin

Dormck
Dabney, Dormck and Wiggles' Slakaduman Adventure
Dormck and the Temple of the Healing Light
Sikado's Star of Aragon

Table of Contents

Preface i
Chapter 1- Simple, Meaningful and Real 1
    We Can Learn from Nature 4
Chapter 2- Intuiting Your Dreams 11
Chapter 3- The 3 Keys to Understanding Your Dreams 23
    The Third Key of Dream Understanding 29
    Summary: Three Keys of Dream Interpretation 33
Chapter 4- People in Dreams 39
Chapter 5- Dreams Can Change Your Life 53
    Blare Magazine 63
    Smitty 63
    Why are the language and symbolism of dreams so strange instead of being direct? 69
Chapter 6- Remembering Your Dreams 75
Chapter 7- Types of Dreams 85
    Lucid Dreams 86
    Creative Dreams 88
    Prophetic Dreams 91
    Recurring Dreams 94
    Nightmares 97
Chapter 8- Our Main Journey is the Journey Within 99
Recommended Books 107

Preface

When I started studying Yoga with Prof. Yogi Bharat J. Gajjar and Shantanandaji, the topic of dreams and their importance came up. Before this enlightening topic was taught to me, I had never paid much attention to dreams or dreaming. I did not learn about the importance of dreams until I was somewhere near 25 yrs. old. The other students and I were taught to allow ourselves to be awakened during the night, keep a pad of paper and a pen nearby to write down first impressions; because when we would awake, the dreams would lift up and go off into the ethers if we didn't. If we would write down parts of the dream, then it helped us to remember the whole dream once we began talking about them.

When I met Chris on the streets of Philadelphia, many years ago, we talked about how I was taught to remember my dreams and discover what they meant. We first started writing down our dreams in journals, recording them on tape and talking about them first thing upon awakening, so we would not forget. Chris had never done this before, but he thought it was a great idea to start. I am glad he did, because here we are 43 years later, sharing all that we have been taught about dreams through our listening to the Holy Spirit.

Once we moved to Doylestown, PA, we happened to live across the street from a community college. Based on the understanding we had acquired through cataloguing and discussing our dreams, we decided to write a book about dreams and their meaning. One night I had a dream that showed me a map of Padanaram. When I awoke, we looked up maps in our biblical bible. We found maps and we found Padanaram, which was an area in modern day Syria, referred to multiple times in the book of Genesis. We were told to remember that name because we would someday use it. Well, someday came. We changed the name to Padaran and used it as the name of our publishing company.

We found we could use the university's typewriter for free and do copying as well in the Student Union. We decided we would make our book using the Student Union as our office. We found out, through inquiry, that the magazine**, Mother Earth News,** would allow us to take a small affordable ads out in it and we began to get orders for our book, **Hidden Manna: How to Understand Your Dreams**, through them.

We had a glossary in the back of the book that would help the dreamer get the gist of understanding their dreams. We were the publishers, the "graphic designers", the authors and the marketing department all in one. We did not have an ISBN number, YET, but eventually we were enabled to learn how to get one through R.R. Bowker. We opened our company, Padaran Publications! Such excitement. Here we are NOW, having published 9 books and now 10 including this one. All are either Best-Selling books or Award-Winning books. They can be purchased through http://www.padaran.com.

We are delighted to share our dream journey with you, the reader, in our updated version of the book that started with such humble beginnings many years ago. Along the way, you will discover methods and techniques that we hope will inspire you to work with your dreams along the path of your journey to enlightenment.

Chapter 1- Simple, Meaningful and Real

"The future belongs to those who believe in the beauty of their dreams."
Eleanor Roosevelt

Many people go through their lives without realizing one of the essential truths about the nature of life; and that is, at its root and at its core, life is meant to be a simple, enjoyable, peaceful and graceful experience; life is meant to be easy, not difficult; life is our Creator living through us with joy and simplicity like that of a child.

We used to believe that life was a struggle, an emotional, mental, spiritual battle where only the strong survive. Your beliefs are a self-fulfilling prophecy; since we believed that life was a struggle, based on that strong belief, that is what we experienced on a daily basis.

In this worldview, you are caught in this fight between positive and negative forces at work in your life. The negatives include fear, hatred, lies, deceit, anger and jealousy. These keep trying to drag you down until you counter them with positive thoughts and emotions that center around love, peace, joy, harmony, compassion and faith. Life is a journey caught riding this mental/emotional roller coaster as these forces battle it out for the fate of your soul. Your daily experience in the external world mirrors this contentious model when you are caught in this struggle.

Simple, Meaningful and Real

As you will see in our book, there is a way out, a way off this unsettling topsy-turvy journey, a way back to the way things are meant to be. You will see that there is a way to step back and see things plainly. There is a way to be guided on the clear and simple path. Our book is written with the hope that you can be sensitized to the inner Voice that leads you down the path of life; to find that effortlessness and peace that comes from understanding yourself as you really are. We are on a journey together to find that place. Dreams will be our guideposts along the way.

We have learned through many years of studying our dreams that they are messages from our Higher Self, our Creator if you will, through His/Her Spirit directing the processes in our unconscious mind, to show us what is transpiring in our inner life. We get an honest, unbiased revelation of our inner world from this source, which reveals that which is destructive in our nature so that we might change; to teach us in the ways of judgment, in getting to know our true Self and weeding out the false voices within so that we may have the ground of truth to stand on.

It is a common notion that dreams are imagined fantasies, "pies in the sky"; that they represent unattainable goals or meaningless nonsense. Our experience runs counter to all these notions. Dreams are truthful in the ultimate sense, grounded in the ultimate reality. They speak to the individual dreamer in such a way that her own true nature is revealed to her. Our part is to diligently record and study the dream and be receptive to the inspiration to see it clearly. Dreams are meaningful and real.

Dreams are records of our inner life, thoughts and feelings about ourselves and others, which reveal the thoughts and intention of the heart and mind in particular situations. Here is an example of a dream story and how we came to understand it.

Chris had a dream that went as follows: "A poor, slum-dwelling man pulled out a knife to threaten me because he was mad at me. At first, I was afraid when he zipped out the razor-sharp zip-blade; but then I became confident when I realized he could not touch me because I am a good fighter. Previously, I had walked through this man's 'house', which was an abandoned building where he was squatting. This had brought his anger on, even though the roadway was blocked and his so-called 'house' was the only way to pass through the area; furthermore, I had passed by unobtrusively trying not to bother him or his wife."

Our understanding of the dream stemmed from an incident that happened the night before the dream, where we had been watching a concert in a nightclub. During the evening, Chris approached a man who was standing in our line of view to the stage and asked him if he would move over, so our view would not be blocked. The man became offended and threatened us with his looks and demeanor, but eventually moved. Chris was intimidated and fearful when he first thought about asking the man to move so our view wouldn't be blocked. Then Chris realized he did not need to fear the man because he was a strong person. At that point, he went ahead confidently with his request for the man to move and did not get shaken when the man responded crossly.

The dream is essentially those inner forces at work within Chris during the time of the incident. He felt resistance about trying to speak to the man at the club, represented by the squatter who was protecting his "house", which was the status quo of a situation having the view of the stage blocked. He experienced fear and intimidation as he pondered asking the man to move, seen in the "zip-blade" and anger of the man in the dream. He found the courage to speak, seen in the dream when realized the man could not touch him because his is a good fighter. The fact that the man was a "slum-dweller" refers to the nature of the spirit Chris was contending with, which is one of low self-esteem and acceptance of a poor situation. These inner forces were going on within Chris and externalized in the interaction with the man, then revisited/revealed in the dream.

There are some important things to note about dreams in general from the specifics of this dream.

The inner (spiritual) condition of people is revealed. That is to say, that which goes on inside the dreamer, his thinking, emotions and feelings are revealed symbolically or directly.

Dreams most often refer to specific events and the inner workings going on during those events. The key to understanding them lies predominantly with the person who has been through that incident. This underscores the transcendent fact that these are personal messages from the Higher Self through the unconscious, contained within the dream.

In line with this reality, it becomes incumbent on you to be more aware of each day's activities and situations, particularly the thoughts and feelings involved, so that the key to understanding the dream will be clearer in mind.

There is symbolic language in the dream which must be understood to grasp the meaning of the dream. For example, the zip-blade represented for us dagger-like hateful thoughts, attitude and intention. The house represented a poor situation or low level of thinking. The slum-dwelling squatter was symbolizing an aspect of low self-esteem and acceptance of a poor situation, which had to be overcome to move forward.

The dream represents something real, something that happened on the inner plane of existence. Chris could have succumbed to intimidation and fear at the nightclub and lost his self-confidence and done nothing. This would have changed the type of dream he received. Or, the man could have generously moved aside from blocking Chris' view in real life and politely apologized for his insensitivity, which would have been reflected in the changed nature of the dream or maybe Chris would not have experienced a dream at all about the incident.

Being awake in consciousness and aware of your inner life are keys to understanding dreams, and keys to living the simple clarity that is our divine inheritance. As we just mentioned, in each moment of our lives there is a need to be aware of what is going on within us so that the inner thoughts and intentions can be harmonious, balanced and well adjusted; in line with our true purpose. Dreams are an ongoing record of these inner workings, like a tape recorder placed inside and turned on within your mind and heart. Those who use their dreams wisely and diligently will find inner strength of spirit and a great storehouse of truth and knowledge about the Self.

We Can Learn from Nature

We can take a lesson from nature to understand the value of dreams in day-to-day life. Nature teaches us that each animal must be aware of its enemies and true to the laws of its own nature, must be aware in order to survive.

Simple, Meaningful and Real

For example, the small deer feeding at a waterhole must be wary of the wild cat prowling nearby; not "sleeping" in this situation, because that could bring on the moment of disaster. Furthermore, the wild cat is regularly on the prowl for weak, unaware prey that can quench his persistent hunger. The trees abound with the warning cries of birds and small creatures that shout out when danger is encroaching on their territory.

Each animal must provide for three basic necessities in order to survive in nature; first, a nest or home to protect it from its enemies, to house its young, to harbor its food, to guard against inclement weather. Second, an animal must be aware of its enemies, whether they are predators, weather or man, and not be overcome by them so that it can survive. Third, an animal must constantly gather food and water to provide the energy it needs to live. Man, likewise, must perform these same vital functions. He must have a home or shelter, for much the same reasons as the animal does. He must be aware of his enemies; not only of those he can see, but also of those he cannot see (invisible "enemies" that exist in the mental/emotional/spiritual realm). Third, he must gather food and water to provide the nourishment his body needs to function, grow and stay healthy.

Life for humanity is spiritual as well as physical. We have a spiritual house, the temple of our body, the home of our mind, the seat of our emotions, to maintain. As in the example of the animal in nature, the spiritual house performs certain vital functions in our lives. It protects us from being overcome by negative thoughts or emotions that would destroy us; it harbors our young, which are the ideas and creative thoughts which sustain life and give it more meaning; it stores our food, which is the knowledge we need to stay alive, vibrant and vital; it guards against inclement weather, which are the emotional/mental trials and tribulations we sometimes can encounter.

The enemies we must watch for in the spiritual sense are the thought forms that would hurt us by keeping us in a type of mental bondage. These thoughts could be caused by doubt, fear, worry, pride, anxiety, frustration, spite, anger, hatred, resentment, lying, cheating, stealing or any of a host of other negative energy forms. We must choose to be on alert against these things since aligning with these low energy thought forms will drain our experience of happiness, peace, clarity and joy that is our natural, God-given inheritance. A useful technique is to affirm the converse if we notice one of these thought forms trying to take root in our mind. A simple example would be when you hear the thought, "I feel terrible", don't resist or fight against it, but affirm "I feel great" with emotion.

In our spiritual life, we are looking for food to be gathered and digested in order for life to be sustained, just as we do in our physical life. What is this spiritual food? What we are examining is the daily bread from "heaven" that many people overlook (as spiritual food), which is the hidden manna of dreams. Just as the children of Israel gathered the manna, which mysteriously appeared every morning, to eat as they wandered through the desert, so every person is provided each morning when we wake from sleep, food for the day to sustain our spiritual life. We can choose to gather this food, ingest it, digest it, or we can choose to ignore it, in which case it will disappear in the midst of daily activity, just as the manna disappeared in the glare of the sun if the Israelites failed to harvest it in a timely manner. It is rare that you will remember your dreams if you don't tune into them immediately after waking, as the concerns of daily conscious living will chase them out of your mind. It does sometimes happen when something you encounter during the day triggers a remembrance of the dream. This is likely because you are experiencing something in your inner life that is related to that dream. What this hidden manna will provide is to reveal the inner happenings of the recent past of which you should be aware, or it will reveal the inner incidents of the coming day as you will face them. This can set you on your way with an awareness, guidance and perspective, strengthened and walking in the flow of your true Self on your daily journey to your Promised Land.

Symbolic language reigns supreme in discussing these concepts. The Promised Land, like the Kingdom of Heaven, is that place where you are living as one with your Higher Self/Divine Mind, freed from the burdens of those emotional/mental patterns that hold you down. Some of the spiritual texts refer to your garments being clean, white as snow, which refers to a spiritual consciousness that has transcended the duality of the ego self, knowing who she is in truth. The Holy Spirit is the mechanism by which the God-mind works in the world to reveal Itself to you. Our garments are our prevailing thought patterns. We can choose to align with this higher reality by harboring thoughts that bear the fruit of the Spirit, love, joy, peace, patience, kindness, goodness, faithfulness, gentleness, and self-control.

We will consider some of the creative and prophetic aspects of dreams at a point later in this book. The dominant element of our daily dreaming has been shown to be what might be called the harmonizing/guidance aspect, the inner guide that represents your daily inner life to you in your dreams. The "real" you exists beyond or you might say transcends time, space and this material dimension. It has been referred to throughout history in many ways, the Divine Self, Christ Consciousness, I AM Presence, Holy Spirit, Atman, but regardless of the term you use, this omniscient awareness never sleeps. While your human self sleeps at night, your omniscient Self scans the recent past or immediate future. From that perspective, it reveals yourself to you in a dream story that tells you what is going on in your inner life. Another way to look at it is to think of the various levels of body that you live in simultaneously. You have a physical body, a mental body, an emotional body, an etheric body and a spiritual body. The dreams are providing you an insight as to what is going on in your mental/emotional body reacting to your experience in the physical dimension as seen from your spiritual body's perspective. The language of the dream is symbolic, meant to be understood by your intuitive nature. Let us continue and explore together the amazing process by which this all unfolds for you daily. We will end this chapter with a dream to show how this process works.

Recently, while contemplating options around retiring, Chris had the following dream. "I was staying in a nice hotel with large picture windows looking out from the room. There was a steep cliff outside where the view sloped maybe seventy-five degrees up the side (ninety degrees being vertical). There was a six-foot-high green concrete wall about five yards out from the hotel. The mountainside cliff had snow on it and loose rocks were falling but being blocked by the concrete wall from crashing into the hotel windows. Then I noticed about two or three rooms down to the left, I could see a large landslide of rocks coming down and crashing over the wall into the room. I looked back in front of my window and there was only an occasional small rock coming down."

The dream continued; "Later, I bought some coffee at a convenience store and was at the checkout line putting in the PIN for my debit card to pay for it. I could not get the password right, though I knew the password. The people around me in the store were people I worked with. I told the cashier, who I knew, I will pay you later if you just cancel the transaction so these people in the long line that had formed can buy their stuff. I walked from there and came to a large conference room where they were setup for a jewelry show and sale. I saw a man I worked with coming out as I was going into the area to find a place to sit down and be quiet."

We considered the dream and came up with an understanding of how it related to what was going on in Chris' inner life. We mentioned that he was working through moving on to retirement and this sometimes seemed to be a daunting transition. Pondering something, inner reflection can be represented by looking out a window in a dream. The seeming difficulties Chris was thinking about in making the transition to retirement were shown several ways, as the steep cliff outside his window, and the difficulty checking out at the convenience store. He had previously discussed with his manager whether to stay on part time or just move on completely from the job into retiring. These and other thoughts around what might happen were represented by the rocks falling from the cliff and the people lining up behind him at the convenience store, feeling pressured by these concerns "lining up" in his mind. Chris' manager informed him, on the day after he had this dream, that he had discussed the option of Chris staying on part time with the CIO and that idea had been put down, so it was no longer an option for Chris. The elimination of this part time work as an option is symbolized by the rocks crashing down into the room several doors down from Chris in the hotel. This was "peripheral" to him because it confirmed to him that he really did not want to continue working. Looking straight out in front there were a few rocks falling (minor concerns if you will), but nothing major since he had thought through his retirement scenario and felt good about it (protected by the wall).

Simple, Meaningful and Real

Chris went through with the retirement and was calling around to venues to try and line up some music gigs several days later. He was talking with the hostess from one place and she mentioned the manager who Chris needed to contact. It turns out this was the same person Chris had seen in the dream when he was walking into the jewelry show. That really struck Chris as rather amazing that his dream would foretell this connection and confirm to him the path he was on, retiring from his corporate job and pursuing his passion with music. We will continue this path of amazement and wonder as we look further into the nature of the dream journey.

Simple, Meaningful and Real

Chapter 2- Intuiting Your Dreams

"I, Daniel was grieved in my spirit in the midst of my body and the visions of my head troubled me. I came near unto one of them that stood by and asked him the truth of all this. So he told me and made me know the interpretation of the things."
Daniel, Ch. 7, v.15-16

We have found that, in order to fully understand your dreams, you must develop intuitive understanding and a spiritual awareness of life, because simply stated, dreams are spiritual messages meant to be understood by your intuitive nature. Let us lay the groundwork for what we mean by explaining the underlying framework of principles and fundamental truths that we have been taught over the course of our dream study.

Dreams reveal, in the form of a symbolic story, what is transpiring in the unseen realm of our inner world, unknown to the physical senses. When sleeping, the blinders that prevent us from seeing the unseen workings of the mind and heart (and spirit) are removed; so that the channels are open without interference for the inner mind to receive messages from the unseen power that underlies all things, what we call the Spirit of God. The unconscious mind is the landscape that the dream creator travels through as it reveals what is going on within you.

Intuiting Your Dreams

The state of mind necessary to receive these inner stories is also found in those whose spirits and minds are open to receive visions and revelations, whether sleeping or in a visionary state. Several things happen when you are sleeping or in the visionary state. You are not attached to the five senses and the distractions that they present. The cares, worries, mistakes, error thinking and burdens of life are removed from your consciousness and you go deep into the ever present Mind so that you are free to receive these messages about the invisible world of your thoughts and feelings.

You can do this brief experiment to get an idea of what we are describing. Sit quietly and look around you, observing the things you see in the environment around you. Repeat quietly to yourself the names of what you see, the chair, the grass, the sky, lights in the ceiling, whatever it is. Ask yourself, am I those things that I am naming? Pretty clearly, you will conclude that you are not those things. Next, look at the thoughts and feelings you have about your environment. Is it cold, warm; are you angry about someone who comes to mind, happy about a baby you see across the room? Ask yourself again, am I these thoughts that I am having about my world? Once again, if you are honest, you will admit that you are not your thoughts. Who is thinking those thoughts? We would call it your conscious self, or another way to describe it is your conditioned mind, conditioned to certain ways of thinking and feeling by all your experiences in this life (or lifetimes it that is your belief). This is your ego self that that is aligned with this material dimension, the ups and downs, yin and yang of existence, duality and feelings of separation. Is this the real you? In the spaces between the busy-ness that your conscious self is experiencing, there is a deeper awareness. If you can learn to quiet all the distractions of your mind and world around you, you can catch a glimpse of this deeper Self. That is the purpose of meditation and deep contemplation. This is the Self that is ever aware, observing the life of the conscious you. Your dreams come to you from this deeper awareness, freed from the material world of time and space, when you release yourself to sleep.

Within every man and woman, there exists this Inner Voice, which we can call the Superconscious or Divine Self, that is unaffected by the distractions of the visible world. The dream view remains steady to this

Intuiting Your Dreams

Inner Voice. The situation is like that of a ship in the ocean; the body of the ship is tossed about by the wind, but the rudder remains anchored in the water to keep the ship safe on a steady course. One of the main values of working with your dreams is that they educate you and guide you on that steady course. They deliver stories, on a daily basis, that tell you in symbolic imagery what is really going on with your inner life, how your conscious self is responding on the inner planes of your existence to the experiences of your life. The philosopher stated, "Know Thyself;" and we have found no better way to follow this guidance than dreams. If you wish for your thoughts, feelings and consciousness to remain clear and truthful on your inner journey, it is necessary to maintain contact with the Inner Voice, the Voice of the heart, the Voice of truth, and not be swept away by the cares and worries of this world or the many distractions and deceptions this world has to offer. The dream view remains an ever-present steady rudder for your soul.

It is for this reason that dreams, as any other workings of the Divine Spirit within us, become so significant. We have had our dreams referred to in the dreams themselves as a magazine, a newspaper, or a TV station. They report daily relating the events in the life of our own inner nature. You may be shown flying in a dream after experiencing elation or euphoria when something went well in your life. You may have a difficult confrontation at work coming in the day ahead and your morning dream shows daggers being thrown at you by an enemy. Dreams catalog our true thoughts, feelings and intents of our heart, recording and replaying these for us to help remain in touch with our Inner Self on this journey of our life, so as to not be fooled into believing that the ups and downs of ego existence are the ultimate reality. Furthermore, they report on our emotional life, revealing the sadness, joy or other emotions to which we might otherwise lose track in the pursuit of our daily lives. As you see your inner life being revealed to you, you begin a process of separation whereby you begin to become united with your true Self and pull away from identifying as your ego self, separating the wheat from the chaff.

It is therefore true that dreams are one of the keys that open the gates to the "Kingdom of Heaven" (our Superconscious or Divine Mind). When Jesus said the Kingdom of Heaven is within you, he was referring, among other things, to the Inner Light of truth that is responsible for the dreams we receive and the understanding of them. He referred to the kingdom of peace and joy within us to which the knowledge of dreams can lead us.

    The ego self tends to gravitate to feelings of negativity, disharmony and separation and holds onto these ways of thinking in a self-fulfilling cycle of highs and lows, negative experiences and unfulfilled living. Unresolved inner debates and struggles lead to more problems and uncertainties that make you susceptible to difficulties, mistakes, confusion and the feeling that things are not working in your life. When you are worried and overly concerned about food, clothing, shelter or work-related concerns, you magnify these issues in your life. These worries and concerns that you focus on become attracted to you and create your reality. Abundant fantasies, daydreaming and imaginings, while they can lead to creative thinking, if overdone, will take you out of the present moment and literally cause you to "miss out" on your life and opportunities as they present themselves. Fear, doubt, anxiety and stress paralyze the positive functioning of the mind and have the effect of instructing the cells of your body to malfunction and generate some type of disease. On top of all this, we live in a world which is constantly manufacturing all types of distractive or negative stimuli for the ego self through social media, the internet, TV, radio, newspapers, cellphones, etc. This mass culture wants to keep you consuming, needing more of everything, feeling fearful, lacking and distracted. Your old, conditioned nature can also be full of pride, unwilling to admit there is a need for change. The human, ordinary mind is constantly bombarded by an array of thoughts and concerns that keep it chained to a mental captivity, a burdensome, heavy existence from which there appears to be no escape. That is, until we turn within and use the tools the Universe has provided at our disposal, like dreams, to reclaim our inner life.

    Dreams come in the form of a story in which the dreamer is either an observer or a participant. They come from the perspective of your Self as you really are, not as you might think you are or be deceived into believing that you are. The dreams reveal what the Self sees when you thought a certain way about an incident in your life; what the Self sees when you interacted emotionally with forces or people in your life. They reveal what you were seeing, feeling, thinking or experiencing as the event to which the dream refers was happening, as seen from the perspective of your inner Self.

As a simple example, Chris had a short dream where he was inside a hotel room on a resort type beach area looking out on the ocean through a big picture window. He saw a wooden walkway-bridge leading out to an island in the bay. There were young boys on bicycles riding out at different intervals one by one to the island. Occasionally, there would be a boy returning on a bike. The problem was that the walkway was very narrow and Chris had difficulty seeing how the boys coming back and the boys going out could pass each other.

We start to understand the dream by realizing that it is being seen from the perspective of Chris' higher Mind. We concentrate and invoke a confident tranquility, beginning to "nail down the corners" of this dream, or, in other words, to find out the parts of the dream that we can understand so that we can unlock its meaning. Immediately, we see that the picture window represents vision, looking out over the ocean, or in this case, inner vision of his emotional landscape. The boys on the bikes represent Chris's thoughts going back and forth, most in one direction, of one type (positive), and some in the other direction, of another type (negative). As it turns out, Chris remembered he was having difficulty seeing how he could reconcile conflicting thoughts about a particular situation on the afternoon of the dream. This train of thought was represented by the walkway, and the problem with the boys on the bikes is representative of Chris' problem with contradictory thoughts. The conflict of thoughts and the dilemma that it presented was being observed by his true Self and "recorded" in the dream. Chris' conscious mind was being tossed about by many thoughts, but his true nature was observing things as shown in the dream.

From the above example, we can begin to see that if a person wished to interpret a dream, she must:

See the dream in the light of spiritual truth (inner reality) and realize that the dream is a message from Spirit (Divine Mind).

Recognize that the dream is a representation of some inner happening in your life or, in special cases, the life of someone close to you.

Unlock the meaning of the dream-story so that the incident, thoughts, feelings or any other internal occurrences to which the dream refers are revealed.

You might have to take something of a leap of faith here, particularly if you have been led to believe that dreams are meaningless meanderings of your subconscious mind, based on physical stimuli or created by your psychological repressions. The last might be closer to the truth if you see your goal of harmony and balance being aligned with what we mean by aligning with spiritual truth. Divine mind is sweeping through the ocean of your unconscious to reveal those things that are causing an impact. The net effect of this effort will be to restore you to your true path and remove those blockages that are standing in the way while showing those inner events that give you joy, happiness and harmony. As you become more focused on what is happening in your inner life, it cannot help but cause a shift in perspective in your conscious living.

There is a bridge being built, which is constructed as you remember and study your dreams, between your conditioned mind and the "unknowable" unconscious realm. This world of duality that we live in is symbolized by yin and yang, but found in the feminine/masculine, inner/outer world and unconscious/conscious aspects of your mind. Your dreams connect these apparent opposites by showing your conscious outer self what is going on within the unconscious inner world. They unite your masculine and feminine natures in the way that you use the combined forces of your intuitive nature and logic to understand the dreams stories. A harmony and balance are struck as your dualistic worlds are unified into a deeper understanding of the nature of your reality. You grow to be in touch with your spiritual nature because there is no duality in Spirit.

Let us review now what you must keep in mind in order to stay on track while you seek to understand your dreams. Then we will talk about the three keys of dream interpretation that are designed to step you through the process of gaining insight and clarity.

First, let us be clear and re-emphasize this. Dreams are messages from Infinite Intelligence, through the medium of the Holy Spirit (Divine Mind), using the vast repository of imagery and experience

Intuiting Your Dreams

available in the unconscious mind. These speak through and to the inner person, who is a spiritual being. Each of us has a true Self, a perfect nature that is a pure spirit in the Creator's image, and your dreams are coming from this Divine source. Because of this, they are pure, unadulterated, pristine, holy and truthful in every sense of these words, not clouded by any of the imperfections and confusion that exist in our material existence; nor do they pay homage to the false masks that our character may have acquired during this life.

Secondly, these messages about your inner life appear as a symbolic story, like a TV show or a movie (we will touch on this later). They express feelings, thoughts and emotions that are unfolding on the inside as a person lives his life. The time period of the dream (most always) refers to something going on that is essentially present (from the day before to the immediate future). This is not to say that dreams can't be prophetic or refer to something in the distant future that causes you to remember the dream when it becomes relevant or have a flashback of the dream when the incident to which the dream refers is happening. Please remember, however, that your ego self would love you to deflect from itself and have you believe that your dreams are great visions of the future, planetary messages, meaningless junk, or anything that would prevent you from looking inside and seeing what is really going on. The subject of the dream is generally something that has been observed by the inner true Self and is seen from the perspective of this Self. The conscious mind of the dreamer may have forgotten the things that are recorded in the dream, but the true Self that is always awake has noticed and revealed them to you.

Third, let us reiterate that all things (images, words, people, action, props, etc.) that appear in dreams are to be understood symbolically or spiritually, not in a literal or material sense. There can be many levels of meaning simultaneously going on in a dream; such as when there is a physical component (a direct message about something in the material dimension), an inner component and a prophetic component, but the main point of emphasis is how it relates to your inner life. Dreams are messages about the spiritual realm, using images from the visible or imaginary world that can be seen to represent things going on in the invisible world that cannot be seen.

For example, functions of the physical body (such as eating, sweating, or urinating, etc.), which appear in a dream could represent the inner counterpart of that function going on in your inner being. When you are eating in a dream, your inner being is being fed something. You need to ask, "what is the quality of the food you are eating?" Does it taste bad? This could represent something emotionally/mentally unpleasant to accept. Does the food taste good, like a gourmet meal? This could be representative of an inner revelation or realization that was pleasing to your spirit. Are you sweating in the dream? Does it come from fear, worry, anxiety, being overworked? These kinds of questions will help you to understand what the dream is trying to show you.

If you are urinating, then you are getting rid of some liquid waste matter from your inner being, which could indicate an emotional release (only the dreamer would know what this refers to specifically, since the dreamer is aware of what is going on inside). This would be experienced as getting rid of bad, upsetting thoughts or feelings about a situation. A window that appears in a dream might be a spiritual window or what might be called inner vision. A car could represent your state of mind or consciousness at the time of the dream since it is the vehicle in which you are moving.

Likewise, a house and the parts of a house that appear in dreams (rooms, appliances, furniture, etc.) symbolize their spiritual counterpart. Opening the door is receiving something into your spirit; closing the door is blocking something out. Cooking a meal could represent pondering over a dream (which is a spiritual meal). The house itself represents your spiritual house or, in other words, your inner being. Your inner being could also be represented, as we have seen in our dreams, as a factory, city, street, or an old neighborhood (old patterns or ways of thinking that you associate with that neighborhood).

The list of examples is endless, as endless as there are ideas or images; but the principle is consistent. We would advise you to consider this principle and develop a spiritual understanding by learning to see material things as representative of hidden truth. This ability to see intuitively/spiritually will be particularly helpful with some of the more "bizarre", seemingly incomprehensible images that might occur in your dreams.

The symbolic nature of the language and imagery of the dream story can be compared to a movie or a play. The director is your Higher Self, the Holy Spirit or Divine Mind directing the show about your inner being, which is the set where the "movie" is being filmed. All the aspects of your inner life can be found in the dream movie/play. The setting represents your attitude or state of mind at the time that the dream refers to. If, for example, you are in a beautiful, beach-like setting, this could mean an elevated, happy, positive state of mind. A dilapidated tenement could represent a negative, depressed attitude. The mood or atmosphere of the dream is more closely aligned with the emotional being or feelings of the dreamer. You might have dreams where there is a pervading sense of fear throughout the whole environment, or in another dream, the ambience could feel light and airy. Tune in to this emotional tenor of the dream and that will help you to lock into the inner incident to which the dream is referring.

The plot is the inner story line; what is going on within you is represented by the actions in the dream. Chris recently had a dream where he was on a large elevator platform open to the outside; he was going up through many floors and the elevator operator kept on moving through most of them which were dark, but every so often he stopped at a floor that was bright, open to the sunshiny outside world, and was called a level. During the dream, they made it up to the third level, where the elevator operator stopped and let Chris off there to go hit some golf balls in the beautiful surroundings of nature, which seemed like a golf course in the late afternoon, with white puffy clouds overhead. To Chris, hitting golf balls is very relaxing, because he does not do it often and he has no illusions of being a good golfer, so he feels no pressure to do it well. The dream is telling him about a time when he was moving toward a goal and he experienced long periods where he was lacking inspiration, then he would have a flash of insight and understanding (the levels) and finally he made it to a point where he released any need to feel pressure and released and let go to enjoy the moment while pursuing his objective (hitting the golf balls).

Another plot line may show you being chased in a dream. This can tell you that your inner being is being "chased" by troublesome problems or thoughts, either within yourself or from those around you. The next step on your part is to determine what these thoughts are. You do this by being honest with yourself and looking within. Most likely, there are more elements of the dream story that can help you to understand them. The key to this understanding lies with the dreamer, as it the case with all the symbolic language and imagery of dreams. Talking it over with someone else can help to unlock this symbolism, but this is for you, the dreamer, to reveal your inner world.

The Holy (Whole-I) Spirit chooses images, symbols, moods and feelings that have a relevance and meaning for you. It is up to you to take the elements of your dream and search for the connecting link that will unlock the meaning of it. If you see an animal in your dream, it is there because it has specific meaning for you and your spirit. A small insect could represent some minor, nitpicking thoughts that you had, whereas an attack by a giant grizzly bear signifies the appearance of a larger issue. Other animals could be akin to "totems" that represent aspects of yourself. You must be free to use your imagination and creativity to uncover the meaning of the symbolic language in your dreams. Remember that they come from the spiritual, creative nature within you and they can only be understood by that same nature. Any heaviness, bad feelings, bad thoughts or other types of negative energy will hamper your ability to understand your dreams. So quiet your mind, focus, pray for answers, be positive and your intuitive Self can go to work understanding the dream message.

You are bound to see people or imaginary beings in your dream story. These are the characters of your inner movie. Their various personality traits, feelings, words and actions are representative, in a symbolic way, of the actions, motivations and intentions going on within you during the incident being portrayed. The key to understanding is to use your faculty of inner reflection to determine what these dreams characters mean to you. Daya used to have several dreams about the actor Richard Chamberlain, who represented to her a wise, caring, nurturing part of herself, because that was the way she saw the characters he played at the time in real life. It was also the way she saw Chris appearing to her as that same caring, nurturing person. Explore the characters of your inner movie and peel back the layers of understanding from your dream story.

Intuiting Your Dreams

Chapter 3- The 3 Keys to Understanding Your Dreams

"Dreams are today's answers to tomorrow's questions."
Edgar Cayce

We were led to discover three main keys that unlocked the door to understanding our dreams. When we first met as street musicians in Philadelphia, we soon discovered that, among other things, we had a strong interest in spirituality and dreams. We were having regular dreams, were baffled by the strange stories they told and did not have much of an understanding about them. Our intention was to figure it out. We had notebooks that we carried with us for this purpose. Immediately when we woke up, we would write down words and visual drawings to represent our dreams. Then over breakfast, or in a quiet place, we would share the dreams with each other. Looking within, we would try to make sense of them and help each other to understand what was being communicated. We were baffled on many occasions, but over time we began to make sense of some of the dream messages. The dreams themselves were our major source of understanding, guided by our intuitive nature that was being nurtured by the dream study, much like the breakfast food was nurturing our body. Along the way we discovered three of the major insights that we found to help us in working with our dreams. Let us share them now.

The 3 Keys to Understanding Your Dreams

The first key that we found was related to faith and concentration, being able to be present in the moment and focused. This refers to your whole being in a state of restfulness and peace while the mind and spirit are focused in one direction. There are no distracting thoughts, no other concerns except total concentration on the dream and the understanding of it. It takes a level of dedication and attentiveness to keep the mind under control, but this is really what is needed. The "still small voice" is not going to speak to you if you are not paying attention, or if you are being distracted by other concerns.

Imagine the human mind as a radio receiver set. In order to receive the signal coming in from a distant station, the receiver must be turned on and it must be open to the frequency of the distant channel. If there are many conflicting signals coming over the airwaves in the vicinity of the desired frequency, the transmission will be garbled and hard to understand.

The human mind that wishes to understand dream language and imagery is like the example of the radio. In the first place it must be "turned on"; which means the mind and spirit must be energized and focused in the direction of understanding the dream. How many people today have trouble learning how to quiet their mind and tune in? This is your first job and you might need to work at it. Techniques such as meditation, prayer, affirmations, being in nature and a tranquil setting can help. There are many excellent books (some mentioned below) or trainings on the subject.

Secondly, your mind must be open to the frequency of the radio wave. In the case of the dreamer, this means that the mind and spirit must be open to hear that quiet voice of the Holy Spirit, Divine intuition, inner guidance, as you, the dreamer, are being gently nudged in the direction of understanding. There must be no "conflicting signals" to disrupt the transmission, which, in this case, would refer to the worries, cares or thoughts of any other kind than those that are concerned with the understanding. The mind must be still, quiet and focused; it cannot be tossed around by a storm of contradictory thoughts.

Faith and concentration are the two main concepts of this first key of dream interpretation; faith because it represents the ability to receive something from an unseen source; concentration, because it represents the ability to direct all of a person's energy in one direction. We are talking about the intensity of inner mental power and freedom from distraction. For more specific direction on concentration and faith, there are many other helpful books, including the classics **Think and Grow Rich** by Napoleon Hill, **How to Stop Worrying and Start Living** by Dale Carnegie, and James Allen's **As a Man Thinketh**.

The second key of dream understanding starts by unraveling what you can understand to get to what you cannot understand. At one stage when we were recording our dreams, we were baffled and perplexed when trying to understand them. At the time, we were faintly aware, if at all, that dreams referred to inner happenings in the life of our mental/emotional body. We looked at external things that were happening to us in our daily lives to find the meaning, such as people we met, places we went and the things we were thinking, doing and saying. We also had started to use a type of code word system in which certain words or images symbolized a certain meaning whenever they appeared in a dream. For example, a bed represented a person's situation, something that you "lie" in; a window represented our vision, the way we see things. The problem was that many dreams made no sense at all if we went strictly with our code word system of interpretation, either because we had no code words to identify or because a strict interpretation by code words was contradictory or meaningless. Also, we could not identify external happenings that related to the dream. It seemed that we were missing the mark by looking at people, places and things outside of ourselves to understand our dreams.

Several things started to converge at that time to help us grow to a new understanding about our dreams. We were growing to see that the source of the problems we had in life was not external, not the people and events outside of ourselves, but it was internal, stemming from wrong ways of thinking. Through study and our own personal growth, we became aware that all that happens to a person in life has its root cause in thinking, which plants the seed that manifests in the external world. Whether for the better or worse, all life is mapped out from the inner world of thought. One obvious outgrowth of this realization was that we began to look inside ourselves to find the understanding of our dreams, into our world of thoughts, feelings and emotions.

Then, amazingly, Daya had a dream about dream interpretation. This is how she recorded the dream:

"Next I recall trying to seek out this foreign woman's help in figuring out something. It seems I had some comic books with me and laid them on the table." (We recorded our dreams in 'comic book' form in our dream journal with hand drawn pictures to describe the imagery of the dream and text bubbles above the heads of the characters describing the dialog and activity of the dream.) The dream continues, "They were all new books. I asked her if she had time to help me. Her foreign husband said, 'No! We have to be someplace soon and should leave now!' I begged, 'Oh, please! Just two minutes with her. She knows everything I need to know.' She said to her husband, 'Maybe you could butter the bread with peanut butter and jelly while I help her, Dear.' He went to the other side of the table and worked on my bread sandwich (bread meaning dream). He was really an expert at spreading peanut butter and jelly. He had a real technique for putting the peanut butter exactly right. She finished helping me and put on her coat to leave with him. I saw all the knives had been used for jelly. I took one that looked clean and put on my jelly over the peanut butter. The foreign fellow said, 'The best way to spread peanut butter on your bread is to fill in the holes with it by nailing down the four corners or edges as you go around.'"

This dream was difficult to understand at first, but we applied concentration and faith and the inner voice spoke to us to shed light on the meaning. The problem that Daya had in the dream that she needed help figuring out was our dreams (i.e. the comics) and how to interpret them. The dreams are also represented by the bread and the interpretation of them by the spreading of peanut butter and jelly on the bread. Remember that dreams are "bread from heaven". The foreign couple represent different aspects of how to work with the dreams. The foreign wife was patiently helping Daya with her comics, therefore representing patience working through to come to an understanding from the feminine side of things. The husband was in more of a rush, but nevertheless ended up spreading the peanut butter and jelly, at which he was an expert; representing a masculine energy which is insightful, if not patient, and has a system that he uses to understand dreams; to add the peanut butter and jelly to make it complete.

The final statement that this foreign fellow says is the key one about dream interpretation. He said, "The best way to spread the peanut butter on your bread is to fill in the holes with it by nailing down the four corners or edges as you go around." We can reword this into non-symbolic language by saying, "The best way to understand dreams is to fill in the gaps that you don't understand by nailing down (or figuring out) the things you do understand as you go through the dream." Like the characters in the dream, you lay your dream imagery out on the table just as Daya put her comics on the table. You patiently work through the images and language. You have insights and glimpses of understanding and you "nail these down." Before you know it, things begin to make sense. If you practice you will become an expert.

This was an especially important revelation to us and for those who wish to understand their dreams. A particular dream may seem to be an elaborate, nonsensical story with no apparent meaning, but you begin to "nail down the corners or edges" or find that which you can relate to an inner happening in your life, then the story will begin to open up and make sense to you.

How do you put this into practice? When you are discussing your dreams with another person and trying to understand them, or, if you are interpreting them by yourself, you will hear thoughts within you mind as you go through this process. Thoughts will flash through your mind about some event or sensation or person. These passing thoughts may seem at first to be insignificant or unrelated to the dream, but do not make the mistake of letting these thoughts pass by unnoticed. These may be the very keys that the Holy Spirit is using to unlock the meaning of the dream for you. First impressions can be significant no matter how meaningless they may appear. If you are in tune with Divine Mind within yourself, you will find that the first impression is most often the right one. Your quiet inner voice is generally not going to hit you like a hammer, but it is going to gently nudge you in the direction of understanding. Once you become aware of thoughts or feelings that relate to the dream you are exploring, something will "click" inside and you will know you are on the right track. This is one of the "corners of the bread" that you are nailing down. It will lead to other clues to unravel the dream story. We urge you to become attuned to your thoughts as you study the dreams and to realize the key to understanding is in those very thoughts. Do not disregard them but explore them and allow yourself to see if they fit the pattern of the dream. Do not get frustrated if this does not happen immediately; rather persist on this course and you will find success.

A good example of the need to be attuned to our thoughts occurred at a time when we were discussing our dreams as we drove along in the car. We were stumped by a whole series of dreams that Daya had the night before, being unable to get any sense of what they meant. After several frustrating moments, Chris heard that he should ask Daya to repeat the dreams. He should listen to his thoughts while she repeated the dreams to see if this would trigger a connection that would unlock the meaning.

Daya came to one section of her dream in which she saw a big mechanical fly with fanlike wings that some church people had erected in their church to draw in the flies that were in the church and kill them. As Daya related this part of the dream, Chris heard that this referred to some aspect of him that Daya had seen. He then made the connection to a series of negative thoughts he had been having and the flies in the dream. He had been trying to "kill" these negative thoughts inside himself. In the process of doing so, he had erected a non-harmonious negative nature inside himself, which is represented by the mechanical fly. This was the biggest fly of all, in this context.

The message of the dream when something like this. Chris was deceiving himself by thinking he was doing right by seeking to weed negative thoughts from his mind without realizing that the real problem was a mechanical, discordant nature that was not flowing in a positive vibration. The church people of the dream represented a self-righteous type of nature that nitpicks at little things, but is blind to the underlying source or root of the problem, that being a nature that is out of flow with the Higher Self in the first place.

As a result of this one thought opening an inroad into the dream, a whole series of connections were made that enabled us to understand the dream. This is a frequent occurrence in the study of dreams and a particularly important one. Simple thoughts about dreams can trigger a chain of associations that makes even the most difficult dream easy to be digested and understood.

The Third Key of Dream Understanding

The third important key of dream understanding is the ability to listen to the "Holy Spirit" that we have been talking about. Other words for it are intuition, insight, sixth sense or the "still small voice". Your intuition is the voice of a higher power that we have likened to a radio receiver that is tuned into the signal being sent from the transmitting station. The ability to listen allows the dreamer to hear "thoughts" and make connections that will unlock the meaning of his dreams.

Imagine that you are a spy working in enemy territory during a war. Messages come to you from your home base over your secret radio, but they come in code, so as not to alert your enemy. After you have copied your messages, you must then decode them so that they can be understood. Dreams are like the messages of this example. They come in code-form as a symbolic story full of imagery; they must be de-coded in order to be understood. It is the ability to listen to your inner Self, Divine Mind or the Holy Spirit that allows you to decode your dreams and relate them to something specific that is going on inside of you. The "enemy territory" is the dualistic ego world that your true Self lives within. The dreams are delivering a message to help reveal your inner self to you and in that sense can be seen as a "threat" to the ego, requiring you to step through to a higher level of understanding in order to interpret the dream. The process of understanding the dream forces you to break through to your spiritual nature so that you can find the meaning.

It is important for you to cultivate the ability to listen to your thoughts. One way to do this is to train yourself to be aware of your thoughts, feelings and emotions during the course of the day. Many of us tend to live our lives as a wild animal out of control, rushing and wandering randomly through a wilderness of mind. We go from situation to situation, from feeling to feeling or from thought to thought, without being aware or in control of what is happening. This is not a healthy way to be, specifically for the person who wishes to get help from her dreams. Conversely, the inner focus will yield benefits as you become aware that there is a "You" that is in control of thought and emotion, a "You" that is aligned with the eternal Now. This "You" is the generator of your dreams as well as the source to which you can turn to help with understanding them.

If you must give an oral report on a book in school, it is important that you read the book and study it before going to class. Likewise, if you wish to understand your dreams, you must become aware of your inner life, your problems, feelings, thoughts and personal encounters. These things are the subject matter of the dreams, just as the book is the subject matter of the oral report in the example above. Daya wrote a book titled, **The Only Way Out Is In: The Secrets of the 14 Realms to Love, Happiness and Success!** This phrase, "the only way out is in," applies directly to dreams. The only way out of the dilemma of what is going on with your dreams is by going within for the answer.

This fantastic process of dreaming goes on within the billions of human souls that inhabit our planet. We are astounded at how this all plays out, the creativity, the insight, the truth, the direction and the amazement at the information that is provided on a nightly basis for the guidance of each and everyone's soul. Another startling realization is how little attention is paid to dreams, for the most part, by the vast majority of people. Sure, there have been and continue to be people and cultures who revere their dreams, but generally dreams are tossed aside or ignored by most people daily. We will spend some time later in the book with information for those who need help remembering their dreams. We hope that you will persevere regardless of how much you remember, cherish every fragment of dream story, and follow your intuition to understand the messages that are being provided daily. We envision a world someday where working with dreams will be as pervasive as reading a newspaper, checking up on a smart phone or watching the morning news, is today.

We have mentioned that the same Intelligence that creates the dreams is the Intelligence within that can help you to understand them. We have wondered at various times why the dream story is often so

The 3 Keys to Understanding Your Dreams

symbolic, involving sometimes fantastic imagery. We think that may be the subject of someone else's book, but for our purposes, it is clear that the development of your intuitive nature and inner direction is a key purpose of your dreams. Through dreams, we are getting a picture of what is important to our Creator, which is the integrity of our inner life. This information is veiled by the symbolic language and imagery because that is going to force you to bypass your ego self and look within to understand it. Your inner creative mind is not bound by the limitations of time and space, so it is going to pull whatever is at its disposal to develop a reflection of what is going on in your inner life. The mental/emotional circumstances of the dream story will correspond to what your conscious being was going through during the time to which the dream refers. Your ability to "listen" will help to unravel this mental/emotional context; You will know when something rings true; you will know when it does not. You will automatically begin to pay more attention to your inner life as you start to relate the symbolism of your dream story to the things you were (or will be) thinking and feeling. You will begin to "see" the connection between things going on inside of you and things appearing in your dreams. Your bounding down the street in giant leaps in a dream will correspond to a time when you were feeling elated. An attack by a group of gangsters that you see in the dream will remind you of when you were being plagued by a series of negative thoughts about some issue the day before. All these connections that you can make will be enhanced by an awareness of your inner self and a reminder to go within. This is a process of growth that happens as you record and study your dreams.

The language of the spheres is different than the language we speak on earth. In heavenly language, a whole stream of understanding is communicated in one overarching message. You receive it all at once. In the earthly language, individual items are joined together to form sentences and paragraphs and you go through them one by one to come to awareness of the concepts being presented. In the celestial language, your mind is opened up and you receive everything all at once, all as one package. Remember that our human language is basically an attempt to name and get an understanding of reality. But what is it that underlies language? What is the reality that you are trying to get at? That underlying reality is what is communicated with the language of the universe. The angels and celestial beings communicate in this way. They present things directly from mind to mind. No need to break it down into individual word packages but instead the transmissions of reality is direct.

The Divine Mind that exists in every being can understand this universal language. If you step outside your human ego, then you will be in the realm of direct understanding.

Let us see how this process works. Chris had this dream recently. He was on a cruise ship that was docked and he was getting ready to disembark. His state room looked more like an apartment. He had to use the bathroom, but someone was using it. A member of Chris' music group also had to use the bathroom. They decided to go the lobby but when they got there, they could see long lines of people waiting to use the bathrooms. They went to the concierge desk in the middle of the lobby and a woman there told them that they can pay for a higher level of service and get to use the bathrooms set aside for those customers. They pay the $25 but then can see the bathrooms with the orderlies standing outside also have long lines of people waiting. The band member wants to go to another large room across the hallway to gamble. You must pay for the higher level of service to do that, but there is no-one in the room anyway and no gambling tables that Chris can see. We ask for a refund of our money since the lines are just as long for the people with the higher paying service. Chris thinks about going to the other side of the ship where there are some single bathrooms along the hallway or going outside the ship to a bathroom, but the dream ends at this point with no real solution.

The understanding of what this dream was about came to us later in the day. Chris was sitting on a bench in front of the house with Daya. They are discussing the dream but cannot make any sense of it. Chris walks down the front walkway to throw out the trash and on his way back he tells Daya, "I put together all my old musical equipment yesterday to trade in at the music store so I could have some value down on the acoustic bass guitar I wanted to buy; but I can't come up with a scenario where trading that in would generate enough equity to make it worthwhile. It might be best for me to come up with another plan and sell the speakers and amp online to get enough money. Even that is uncertain though since the Fender amp and Arts and Luthier guitar are worth much more to me than I would get by selling them. I can't come up with a scenario that makes sense." Daya responded, "That is what your dream was about. I can see the connection of you being stymied trying to get rid of (go to the bathroom) of the equipment. All the different scenarios you were going through in your mind were the attempts to come up with a workable solution to go to the bathroom or in other words, find a plan to release the old equipment. The band member (ties in with the musical theme) wanting to gamble in an empty room is the idea of trying to make it work at the music store which had no merit. There was more cost to you (paying for supposed higher level of service) to trade in at the music store, but it would not get you what you wanted. Similarly, selling online was not really going to work either, though you wanted it to."

Notice how dreams encapsulate a mental/emotional experience by symbolizing the inner dynamics at work in you at the time to which the dream refers. If you go into the weeds of minute detail you might miss the mark trying to draw an exact correspondence and never get to the heart of what the dream is revealing. Rather, seek to capture the essence of the inner dynamic that you are/were facing. In the case of the dream above, the key essence being revealed is the sense of frustration at the multiple attempts to find a way to release the musical equipment profitably that Chris was experiencing.

Summary: Three Keys of Dream Interpretation

Faith, concentration, intensity of mental power in a state of relaxation.

"Nailing down the corners of the bread." Finding some element of the dream that you can identify; i.e. a person, place, object, emotion, action or code word; finding the feelings, emotions, thoughts or inner incidents to which the dream refers. Then you know what occurrence the dream refers to and then can go on to understand the rest of the dream from there. Ask yourself, "what is the message?"

The 3 Keys to Understanding Your Dreams

Intuition, insight, the "still small voice" of Spirit, sixth sense, listening power.

Use the three keys to unlock the meaning of the dream and relate it to something going on in your inner life.

The proof is in the pudding, as they say, so let us conclude our chapter by going through some simple samples of dreamlike scenarios and present some possible interpretations of what is going on. What questions should you ask as you try to understand this symbolic "movie" about your inner life? Your dream symbols are unique to you alone, but if you work with these examples, you get a sense of how it works.

Questions to ask myself:

What action is going on?
Example A- I was tuning my guitar.
Example B- A gang of young hoodlums attacked me.

What does it represent?
Example A- Tuning the guitar. This represented my attempts to get my thoughts and spirit back in balance- to get in harmony with myself.
Example B- Young hoodlums attacked. This represented that I was overcome by many thoughts about immature things; worry about my looks, feeling threatened, a low self-image. These thoughts are the young punks in the dream. The young hoodlums symbolize a gang of thoughts revolving around emotions of feeling threatened and under attack. You look within to determine what those thoughts are.

What characters are there? (People, animals, imaginary creatures like a mechanical fly).
Example A- Your bossy aunt.
Example B- A ferocious grizzly bear.
Example C- An angel-like creature with light emanating from around her.

What do these represent?
Example A- Something within you is trying to oppress you or boss you around; perhaps you are doubting yourself or accusing yourself of not being who you could be. What does your aunt bring to mind and how

do you feel about this person? This will help you understand where this is coming from.

Example B- A ferocious bear represents some animal instinct that came at you from within, perhaps triggered by an interaction that you had. Fear or anger thoughts could be represented here.

Example C- The angelic being most likely represents a time you were feeling elevated spiritually in contact with your feminine side.

What objects or places are there in the dream?
Example A- A luxurious, opulent mansion.
Example B- A dead tree with withering branches and leaves.
Example C- A radio blasting rock and roll music.

What do these represent?
Example A- Your higher consciousness, your elevated awareness; such a dwelling place is the inner spiritual you, existing in the beautiful surroundings of your inner being.

Example B- The dead tree is an idea or project of yours that has no life, no lasting value. You can look within to see exactly what this refers to.

Example C- The loud radio, if considered offensive, would be disharmonious, aggravating thoughts and feelings about a situation in your life. Others might consider this to be feelings of exhilaration and excitement if this is what moves the needle for them.

What feelings, atmosphere or emotions are there?
Example A- A feeling of terror pervades the dream.
Example B- You see a man who is elated and happy in a dream.
Example C- A dream takes place on a cold, dark city street.

What do the atmosphere, feelings or emotions signify?
Example A- You are locked in an emotional climate of fear and terror related to a decision or situation in your life.

Example B- The man you see is a part of you rejoicing about an incident in your life. Look at your recent experiences or to the near future and you will see yourself reacting like the man in the dream to something that happens.

Example C- This setting suggests tension (cold), negativity (darkness), and fear or feeling the presence of danger (dark city street). This is a situation that has these factors at work within you.

How do you relate to the characters and action in the dream?

This concerns you as you appear in the dream if you appear at all. Are you an observer? Are you passive or active? Are you being used or are you in control in the dream? Are you fighting, playing or fleeing? These all tell you about yourself as you are in relation to your thoughts and feelings.

Example A- You are fighting in a dream against many Ninja warriors.

Example B- You observe only and never appear in the dream.

What does your position in the dream tell you about yourself?

Example A- The fight is an inner struggle. Your energy and thoughts are upset and in turmoil and you are besieged by warriors skillful in the art of hiding and killing. These thoughts are hard to discover and they are very ruthless in bringing you down and causing your inner turmoil.

Example B- Being an observer means you are more aware of the things going on inside of you as opposed to being a character in the dream, in which case you might not be as aware of what is going on in your inner life at the time of the dream. The dream is always about your inner life on some level, but your level of observation, detachment or action being presented shows how aware, involved or oblivious you might have been to these inner happenings.

Having looked at the various aspects of the dream, you should be ready to translate the dream parable into something that you can understand and have that "AHA!" moment of understanding. To sum it up, let us present an example of short dream that Chris had.

"In the dream, I was trying to pull my car out into the street. It was parked between two other cars that were jammed in so tight I could hardly get out without smashing the other cars out of the way."

The 3 Keys to Understanding Your Dreams

When I looked at the dream, I understood that I was trapped between two ways of thinking that were immobilizing me. I was trying to break free and get moving again. The two ways of thinking that were trapping me were worry about my impending adoption of a child and my continual thinking about forming a musical group. I was feeling angered because I was hemmed in unable to make decisions. Since I could not get clarity and make up my mind my anger was taking over and making me want to "smash" these problems out of my life. Obviously, with the help of this dream I was able to gain perspective, step back, breathe and allow things to work themselves out, which they did beautifully. Our adopted child is now a wonderful 28-year-old young man and we had a great run with the musical group in question.

The 3 Keys to Understanding Your Dreams

Chapter 4- People in Dreams

"And it shall come to pass afterward, that I will pour out my Spirit upon all flesh; and your sons and your daughters shall prophesy, your old men shall dream dreams, your young men shall see visions."
Joel, Ch. 2 v 28

You will find that understanding the people who appear in your dreams is key to understanding your mental and emotional life. Hidden in the symbolic language are characters who appear on the stage of your inner world, acting out the roles that you play within, speaking the words of your inner dialogue, expressing the emotions that you feel by who they are and what they do. During our dreaming, we have seen a huge number of people in the dreams, from our closest friends and relatives, to obscure, barely remembered acquaintances; from famous actors and actresses, artists and politicians to fictitious unknown people. We have been seduced by some in the dreams and brutally attacked by others. Some of our encounters have left us emotionally drained and shattered. Some of them have raised us to great heights. Through it all, we have come to understand that the meaning of these dream characters can be understood by realizing how you see the qualities of who they are, what they represent to you and how you are reacting to them within the dream.

People In Dreams

It is clear to those who have been reading with us on this dream journey together that we have established that your dreams deal with the inner happenings of your life. Inside each of us there is a world as vast as the cosmos, because conscious thoughts are ever changing, new experiences are constantly presenting themselves and emotions are reacting to circumstances. Furthermore, there is our unconscious mind where the thoughts, feelings and memories of a lifetime(s) are stored. This inner universe is in a continual state of evolution as the life of each individual unfolds.

The superconscious mind (Holy Spirit) draws on conscious thoughts and the memories stored in our unconscious mind to present dream stories that represent the workings of our mind and heart. From this vast source of memory, experience and imagination, people are chosen to appear in the dreams. There is something about the person in the dream that expresses what is going on inside of us, the dreamer. We repeat this idea because it is an essential concept to understand and remember. Whether the person in the dream is fictitious, imagined, obscure or contemporary, nevertheless, her presence is key to something going on within us, in our thoughts and emotions.

As you evolve in your dream journey, you will grow from being virtually unaware of your inner life to being fully enlightened about your inner world. These dream people will be your guides on this journey. Let us begin this process by exploring the hows, whats and whys of the influence that people have on your inner life. People can and do affect the way that you think, act and feel. Parents, relatives, family, friends and authority figures, for example, can be living inside you in the form of thought patterns and emotional responses that you exhibit daily. You are trained from an early age to think a certain way, believe certain things and respond with certain emotional patterns. You think that this patterning is the "real" you, but really it is nothing more than an amalgamation of experience and training. In a psychological sense, we might call this patterned self your part of your ego, which has a life of its own within you, but we could hardly call this the real you. The dream people you see are facets of this ego reacting to your daily inner life which are revealed during your nighttime of dreaming.

People In Dreams

So really, the key is to understand what the people who appear in your dreams represent to you about your inner life. So that you may do so, you must be willing to take a step back from your ego and observe yourself from the perspective of your Higher Self, a process that is analogous to what is happening in your dreams. Your "inner" eyes must be open and the light must be turned on inside of you. This is so you can be free from being ruled by the emotional/thought patterns that you might have inherited from different people and situations. Not all the people who appear in your dreams will represent these ego patterns; but as you go through the inner journey of discovery through dreams, you will encounter them. Your dreams are a superb way of turning on the inner light; for revealing the different spiritual energies that could be affecting you.

Once these energy patterns are revealed to you, it is up to you to complete the process of freeing yourself from their influence so that you can attain freedom and independence in your mind and affairs. This process is achieved as you desire to grow and believe that you can. Then you become diligent in applying the information gathered from your dreams and the people who appear in them. As you practice working with your dreams, it becomes a process of inner reflection that will become part of daily living for you.

The people who appear in your dreams would generally represent thought patterns, emotional responses or conditioned thinking occurring in the recent past or the day after the dream. You can help yourself to understand your dreams if you begin to observe your reactions to situations and keep note. Observe the people in your life and determine how they might have influenced the way you think about the events in your life and how you react emotionally to the circumstances in your life. If need be, reflect back to your past and events that might have shaped your inner landscape will be revealed to you; the people who appear in your dreams will be the actors representing these inner forces in your life, your inner mental and emotional states.

For example, imagine that you have a relative in Ohio. In the dream, you appear in his house, talking with him. In conscious life, let us say you have no way to get to Ohio or be in the house of your relative. So there appears to be a problem in understanding what the dream is trying to show you; so how do you make sense of it? First, you must begin to ask yourself questions about your relative so that you can understand his presence in the dream. What type of person is this relative and what stands out in your memory about him? Do you hold him high regard or rather dislike him? What is positive about him as a person? What is negative? Is there anything about his occupation or position that is significant? Most importantly, how does he appear to you in the dream? Is he an enemy, friend, liar, seducer, impediment or a guide? How was he dressed and how did he carry himself?

When you become practiced at this method, you will intuitively feel what it is about your relative that is significant. If you have been observing your conscious life, you will begin to draw a connection between your relative's appearance in the dream and a mental/emotional response that you experienced in your waking life. You will become better at this process as you begin to ask questions and reflect on your inner world.

Once you have a clear picture of your relative's thinking, his spirit and his personality, this information can help you to pinpoint the incident or thoughts to which the dream is referring. He will represent a way of being that is living inside of you that is like his way of being. Ask yourself the questions, "How have I acted or thought like this relative of mine in the recent past?"; Or "What is it about this relative that stood out in the dream?" Also, in many cases, dreams refer to inner events to come in the immediate future, so you may not have yet experienced the event to which the dream refers. If you cannot locate or relate to the appearance of the relative in your dream, then be on the lookout during the near future; usually, later on that same day. In any case, there is something about that "spirit" represented by your relative and his qualities as a person that your inner self has noticed (or will soon notice) in your life's circumstances. This is being shown to you for your inner growth, for balance and harmony in your inner life. This can be understood by searching inside.

In this sense dreams are like a compass that help to guide the ship of your life through the mental/emotional waters of existence. They show you where you have been and where you are going on your inner journey. We have been working with our dreams for a long time, but it's still mind-boggling to think about this tremendous power within you that is not bound by time or three dimensional existence, which has a direct link to your "divine" Spirit, has the vision of higher consciousness and shines like a laser beam of truth on your inner life. Like the captain of your inner ship, you must take the steering wheel to follow the course that is being laid out by your dreams.

You might encounter resistance within you. There is a nature, an "old" nature we have mentioned that is aligned with your ego, which is accustomed to thinking a certain way, feeling a certain way and acting in a certain way. This ego nature might be rubbed the wrong way by what you are being shown in your dreams. As you sit in the theater of you mind and view the actors parading on the stage as they appear in your dreams, there might be a part of you that doesn't want to delve in and understand what is going on. This new dream perspective can be a bit shocking when you first begin to experience the bright light that is shining on your inner world. However, we hope that you realize that your understanding and growing from your dreams is the true path to liberation that your soul has been longing for.

In a dream Chris had this morning, he was given an assignment that he had to accomplish. He was in a busy airport area and began to mingle with the strangers there, having light conversations, joking and getting acquainted. After a while, he remembered the assignment and it dawned on him that it was time for him to travel on. He could not remember where his suitcase was. There was luggage in big piles all throughout the airport area. Chris walked through the area and amazingly found his suitcase. He stepped out of the airport and found himself in a big open area with large fields separated by areas with trees, much like a golf course. He was on a path with another man who was almost like a guide, giving advice. They walked on a path in the center between two fields for a while. They looked off to the left and the man noticed a fire burning two fields over. He commented on it and then ran off and put out the fire. Chris looked ahead on the path, then saw a train track horizontally across the fields and people clustered in an area at the end of the path waiting for the train. Chris moved off to go wait to catch the train and dream ended.

When Chris woke up, he lay in bed mulling things over, half awake, half asleep. He was not directly thinking about the dream, more interested in looking forward to the day ahead and charting a course of activity. One thing that stood out was that he needed to work on finishing the writing/editing of this book you are now reading. He was on vacation and he had time on his hands, but he had been distracted by other concerns and had not made any headway on the book. He had previously set a goal to have a rough draft of the book finished by the end of the year, but these many other concerns had taken up time and impeded his progress. Once Chris was awake, he went to the kitchen and shared his morning's dreams with Daya.

While he was telling this dream above to Daya, he realized that the assignment in the dream was this goal of his to finish the Hidden Manna book. The people in the airport and the conversations with them were the many "concerns" that were distracting Chris from the primary goal of working on the book. He lost his suitcase, which represents losing the focus he needed to be working on the Hidden Manna book. He found the suitcase though (in the piles of other luggage-i.e. concerns) and moved on. Chris has been having a productive day with this book today, writing the very words you are reading now.

Let us talk about the man who is like a guide that appears in the dream, and the people at the train station. The man is "on the path" with Chris. He is a part of Chris that is staying focused on following through with the assignment of working on the Hidden Manna book. The open fields represent the vast open expanse of information that is capable of being presented by a writer, divided by trees which can symbolize an organizational process going on within Chris to process this information and bring it to the page. Chris became briefly angered by something that came up during his day, but regained control quickly and got back to working on the book. This is symbolized by the man in the dream who ran over to put out the fire.

Finally, the people in the train station are those parts or thoughts within Chris that are ready to "catch the train" and go to work on the book. The train has a momentum, a fixed destination and a sense of inevitability as it moves down the track. This harmonizes with the clear purpose which Chris brought to his day as he began to work on this book.

People In Dreams

One of the astoundingly beautiful aspects of dreams is that they are like creative works of art. They can be understood on many different levels. The people who appear in the dreams are like the characters in literature that you studied in school. You need to look deeply into their motivations, characteristics, statements, actions and positioning to understand what they represent for you. Which part of your inner self is being represented by the dream character? As you encounter the people of your inner life in dreams, they are messengers of states of mind and emotions that are bringing you closer to inner harmony or leading you away from it. The clear light of dream awareness pulls no punches. You will see aspects of your inner being represented in ways that may not be flattering, but ultimately if you learn from it, you will be led to greater awareness, greater freedom, greater peace, greater happiness.

Exemplifying this "brutal" imagery that can happen in dreams was an example from a dream Daya had recently. She had a dream of having been raped, but it was not a physical rape. A detective wanted to go over the incident again and again, but she did not want to. She was clearly disturbed about it and saddened. The dream ended.

Later that day she realized her pocketbook and all its contents were missing. She realized that she had left it on the floor in the back of the car when we returned from teaching her yoga class. We looked all over for it trying all possible thoughts of where it could be, but it was not to be found. Chris called all the credit card companies to cancel the cards that were in the pocketbook; Daya texted to stop payment on her check she had received from the yoga center for teaching. The pocketbook itself had great significance for her because we had bought it at a shop in Malibu on one of our trips to California. It was one of a kind and she loved it. It carried the association with those pleasant memories. We eventually concluded, after many attempts at figuring out where the pocketbook was, that it was stolen from the car in our driveway. Chris had gone out to get his coffee from the car and apparently forgot to lock it, though to his mind he had done so in typical ritualistic fashion. Regardless of how it happened, it was gone.

If you have ever had something that means something to you stolen, you realize the sense of violation that it represents. This is symbolized by the rape in Daya's dream. The detective character represents a part of her going over and over in her mind as to where the pocketbook was and what might have happened to it. The whole experience disturbed and saddened her, as shown in the dream. Notice how this event to which the dream refers happened after the dream itself, following the dream later in the same day. Wrap your head around this prescient ability of your dream consciousness to forecast what is coming for you on the inner plane of existence.

Dreams present no illusions about who you are through the people that appear in them, just the truth. The truth is for weeding out your true Self from the many foreign voices that have become a part of you as you have grown up. For example, when we first started dreaming, Chris had many dreams in which his mother appeared. We initially thought these dreams referred directly to his mother and her actions, but it soon became apparent that this was impossible since she was living 350 miles away and we had truly little contact with her at the time. Then we received the understanding that Chris was carrying his mother's "spirit" within him by thinking like her and acting like her. In several dreams, she was shown worrying about circumstances and fretting. As we studied these dreams, we could see the link between the patterned thinking about circumstances in his life that related to this worrying in the dream. These patterns were analogous to the way his mother tended to worry about events. Because of this tendency, she became the perfect character for the dream consciousness to show Chris how he was behaving, having internalized a similar thinking/emotional pattern of worry as that represented by his mother.

Our experience bears out the logic that says that our closest relatives and friends are those that affect us the most and whose effect is the most lasting. It follows that when you first begin to study your dreams you will often see these people appear as characters in them. Regardless, your dreams will lead the way and show you the inner characters who are at play in your inner world.

You begin to step back from yourself a bit, gain a new perspective. Chris found the knowledge about his mother appearing in his dreams to be of great benefit, although troubling at first. It allowed him to see that this type of worrying behavior was not part of his true nature, but rather a way of thinking that he had picked up unconsciously and grown accustomed to, as shown by the mother character and behavior being repeated over and over in his dreams at the time. This process of working with his dreams began to separate him from that worrying nature as he became aware of it, and to bring him more in alignment with a trusting nature, which in turn is more aligned with his true Self.

In effect, your dreams are a source of information, a daily newspaper or spiritual food for the morning, if you will, about what is going on in your inner life. As you study the dreams, you can take this information and separate the wheat from the chaff in your mental-emotional experience. This is spiritual consciousness, to become aware always of the "foreign" voices within you and at the same time learn to know the true voice of your inner Self. Your dreams will show you when are veering off course or moving back to truth.

As an example, Daya had a dream where she was dancing in a regal setting with a famous leading male actor. This dream represented on one level the positive feelings she experienced from a night of talking and sharing intimate thoughts with Chris. Daya had told Chris what she perceived in the actor's persona. A few of the items were that he and Chris appeared similar in personality, had similar traits and she saw both as very handsome. The actor in the dream is symbolizing Daya's feelings of fulfillment in connecting with her inner male self and with her husband Chris as well, who carries a similar energy with him.

You can be trapped into misinterpreting the people who appear in your dreams, however. We had one problem related to this that occurred early in our study of dreams. We were being fooled into flattering ourselves about the nature of the people who appeared. Chris was interpreting his father or other similar authority figures who appeared in dreams to be representative of an angel, Divine Being or the voice of God as it would be speaking to Chris. As this went on for a while, it became apparent that something was wrong with this understanding. As we discussed this together, Daya began to see that these authority figures represented no more nor less than traits and qualities that were like their own, that were at work within Chris. Perhaps our view of the nature of God was growing and that freed us from seeing the Divine in the limited sense as a father figure or authority figure. We were becoming awakened to the fact that people who appear in dreams represent their own nature in the context of the dream. We want to pass on this awareness so you will also be honest in your assessment of the people who appear in your dreams, so you can accurately relate and understand how it applies to your inner life.

Another significant element of the people in dreams concerns what they are doing in the dream. The activity of the person represents some type of mental-emotional activity going on within you, something that is affecting your spirit. The man who is working hard would represent something different from the man who befriended you. In all cases, you have feelings or impressions of the people that appear to you in much the same way that you have impressions or feelings about the people you meet in real life. These personal impressions are a key to understanding the spiritual import of these dream characters.

If you put together in your mind the nature of the person in the dream, your impressions of that person and the activity that is presented, you should begin to get a good idea of what is going on that your inner being has noticed to record in the dream. You can combine these logical elements of understanding with your intuition to complete the picture.

Here is another example from one of our dreams. Chris had a short dream where a man was sitting at a bar and he was all upset; he did not know what to do. He was combination of two people Chris knew from college; one of them was a genuinely nice guy, but he was weak and used by other people. The other was friendly but disorderly and wild, tending to drink too much. In the dream, this "combination" man was sitting at the bar, unable to decide what to do. He thought he might go to Grand Central Station in New York City.

In order that we can understand this dream, let's first look at the qualities, impressions and activities of the "combination" man. It is something that Chris is observing inside of himself. Immediately, we can see that this character represents a split nature, one side that is harmonious ("nice") but weak, the other side that is disorderly even though friendly. We can interpret this friendliness to mean familiarity, the opposite of overt hostility. It is the latter disorderly nature that feeds on Chris' weakness to cause his spirit and mind to be upset, as represented in the dream. The setting is a bar, where people often go to "drown their sorrows", which in this case falls in line with the man being upset, despairing, not knowing what to do in the dream.

Finally, the character decides that he might go to Grand Central Station in New York City, which is a busy, bustling, often confusing place for the individual traveler. Combined with the other elements in the dream, we can see that Chris' inner self was upset and confused and he was contemplating a further degree of related mental activity with bustling, busy thoughts and a state of further worry and anxiety. We can also see that a disorderly spiritual force was working on his inner weakness to create such a state of mind.

Chris remembered how he had been worried and perplexed about a situation in his life the day before this dream. He was worried, feeling out of control, feeling powerless and his mind was wandering all over the place without resolution during the time in question. His dream was making him aware of these inner goings on. This showed Chris the many emotions and influences that were directing the course of his inner self during the time to which the dream refers. The dream helped him to step back and view this inner drama from the perspective of his Higher Self who was directing the dream story. The "video camera" of inner vision was revealing these inner forces at work.

The mechanism at play here is that your Higher Self, God-Consciousness, Christ nature, whatever term you choose to use, is constantly at work to restore balance and harmony in your inner life. Dreams are one of the many ways that this mechanism communicates with you if you are willing to take the time to listen and consider. What priceless knowledge is available here to reveal to you that path to Oneness with your Creator. To the person who is out of touch with himself and his Creator, the Holy Spirit will shine a light through your dreams on the true workings of your inner life, so that you can take that knowledge and restore yourself to balance and harmony. When you are living in harmony with universal law, your dreams will also reflect this reality and you will be receiving affirmations of your direction in the dream stories.

We can say that dreams are messages from the Spirit of God dwelling within man, recounting the true nature of his spiritual life, whether in balance or out of balance. The state of your spiritual condition at the time of the dream will determine the content of the dream. Likewise, the people who appear in your dreams will represent the inner "characters" that populate your inner world, the forces at work within you as you have lived through the events documented in the dream. All the complexities of the human mental/emotional drama are captured in the dream story.

These spiritual influences are very subtle and often go unnoticed by the conscious mind during daily living. However, your higher Self notices all things and as you grow in awareness, you too will notice the significance of your thoughts and emotions that are represented by the people in your dream stories. You will become aware of the spiritual weight that is determined by how you react to the people and circumstances of your life. Thought forms such as worry, fear, anxiety, nervousness, weakness and despair are constantly being passed from one person to another in the world and as long as you are unaware, you will be subject to these subtle influences that you encounter daily. However, as you study dreams and become aware of your mental, emotional and spiritual inner life, you will transcend, deflect or generally be protected from these negative influences through your mindfulness.

After all, what are we all looking for but to be peaceful, happy and loving as we live our lives? As you send out these positive, loving vibrations in your inner life, your dreams will catalog these changes and so your dream stories and dream characters will reflect your elevated consciousness. The dreams show us what is actually happening in the spiritual realm, so as we grow and study our dreams, we become much more aware in our daily lives; aware enough to shut off the negative influences seeking to find their way inside and aware to open our hearts to positive influences inside ourselves. We become much more aware of negative thinking and its effect so we can deter it; and we become more attuned to the work of our Divine Self so we can receive it.

So, to sum up, let us state the general principles about people in our dreams that we have discussed in this chapter.

First, we have stated that people in dreams represent thought forms, "invisible" emotional energy influences that are in control of your inner life at the time of the dream. Second, we have indicated that these influences are primarily found within you at the time the dream refers to

People In Dreams

(and there is a rare exception where dreams show you something going on in someone else's inner life). The way to interpret the nature of these characters is to study the character traits and qualities of the person represented, be aware of your impression of the person and consider the activities that are happening in the dream. Through faith, combined with concentration, you can intuitively relate these to something happening in your inner life.

People In Dreams

Chapter 5- Dreams Can Change Your Life

"The biblical concept of divine Word (logos) suggests an analogy taken from contemporary science. The communication of information is an important concept in communication theory, computer networks, and the DNA in organisms. In each case communication requires selective response (decoding) and the interpretation of a message in a wider context..."

From <u>When Science Meets Religion: Enemies, Strangers or Partners?</u>
Ian G. Barbour, Harper San Francisco, pg. 61

Regardless of how interesting and fascinating dreams may be, they become tremendously valuable where the rubber meets the road, which is to say when you learn how you can use your dreams to change your life, to grow and to help discover who you are. It is time to dedicate some time to the process of discovering more about how these monumental cornerstones of divine communication can be used in daily living. We will start with an excerpt Chris wrote (in the first person) about how dreams helped him to turn his life around. He wrote this in the draft version of the book many years ago.

"As I look back over my study of dreams and the thousands, multiple thousands of dreams I have had, there are two dreams that stood out as keys to my growth and development as a whole person. These dreams have helped to shed light on other dreams. They have opened large doors inside of me in my pursuit of self-awareness.

The first dream was one that Daya (my wife) had. She was walking along with a fellow who had just seen her use the power of her word to cast a lustful man into a pit in the name of Almighty God. She called this fellow the 'onlooker'. He wanted to know how she put the 'whammy' on people (meaning casting them out of her presence so they could not harm her in the dream). As they walked, a grungy old man accosted her. He demanded that she help him. She pushed him aside away from her. He then grabbed her from the front. She warned him against proceeding any further, but he kept coming at her. She jabbed her foot into his gut and threw him over her head by grabbing his right hand. He slammed onto the ground with a loud thud.

He wore a dirty, scruffy old overcoat. His skin was diseased from the inside of his body to the outside. He had the thickest tongue she had ever seen. The onlooker told him to open his zipper and show her what his problem was; he told the man to get a facecloth. Then, they both came up to Daya again and said the man needed help from her. She said if you don't really need help, then the Almighty God will deal with you. She told him she wasn't fooling around. She asked him to show her what he had in his possession and he gave her a tube of toothpaste, which had our address on it. She told him to take everything out of the boxes he had with him. He had a bottle of Listerine mouthwash too."

That, in a nutshell, was the dream. We studied the dream and at first, we were baffled by what it could mean. Using the methods we had learned previously, we concentrated, prayed and listened. It started to dawn on us that this man Daya saw was a representation of Chris' spiritual/mental/emotional condition. The dream was showing how her inner self was reacting to dealing with this. The clothes he wore were symbolic of Chris' thoughts, at times old, negative and tainted. His face represented Chris' countenance and his outlook on life. The old, conditioned self in Chris didn't want Daya to help him get rid of his lustful nature, symbolized in many ways in the dream, but didn't know how and didn't want to go about it in the right way with Daya. The onlooker was a more helpful nature in Chris who wanted this 'lustful' side of him to be cured. That is shown by how he knew what the old man's problem was and how to talk to him. The old man was too embarrassed to ask for help so he tried to demand it from Daya and got nowhere until he proved without a doubt that he meant business about getting help.

The term 'lustful' when used in a dream can refer to coveting many things, such as being overly attached to sex, negative thoughts, negative personalities, greed and being defined by your ego self. Whatever drives or compels you to step outside your spiritual nature is 'lustful' in the way we are using the term. So Daya was feeling attacked, as shown in the dream, by inner forces that were trying to make her feel vulnerable and susceptible to going along with the negative thinking Chris was directing toward her. There was a part of her that stood up strongly for herself and her spiritual understanding.

From Chris perspective, he was at first resistant to this interpretation which showed this undesirable side of himself. It pained him to think that he could be shown to be so "ugly". As he looks back now, he can see that his ego had its own image to protect and was reluctant to accept the truth. He had an image of himself as a good person, so how could he accept this undesirable version of himself? But as the dream sank in and he overcame his resistance, he began to see that he was not genuinely happy with himself. He was not in control of his life. His thoughts were often colored in a negative light and he was often worrisome, anxious or depressed. His ego was subject to being taken over by a host of adverse mental states, which included lust, anger, pride, self-righteousness, illusory fantasy, greed, fear, doubt, guilt, indecision, a low self-image and so on. The dream showed him the true condition of his inner self which Daya had been dealing with. He began the work of overcoming his false ego, his false image of himself so that he could find the true 'Me', find peace and inner strength by being rid of those things that were making him unhappy inside. Not unusual to anyone who is ruled by ego, this dream was a wake-up call.

A second dream also stood out at the time for Chris. In this dream, he was trying to find an old friend of his with whom he had shared many experiences, including travelling across the country together. Chris was driving in a taxi in the dream. As Chris followed his friend, he went underground into the subway tunnels like the ones in Philadelphia where Chris played music as a street musician at one time. The walls were dirty and dusty, it was dark inside there, there was trash all over and the scene what like something those of you who have been in a similar subway tunnel can imagine.

Chris followed him through those tunnels, twists and turns and soon the cab driver that was with him told him that he would have to leave. His friend had been out of sight for a long time, but Chris followed thinking he might find him. Gradually, however, the scene began to change. He was no longer travelling through grimy subway tunnels, but now he was travelling through giant hallways with elevated ceilings. The walls and ceilings were made of pure white marble, flecked with sparkling gold and neatly polished. The floors were also polished. Chris peered into one room off to the side where there appeared to be a meeting of prosperous businessmen in suits and ties. The room was decorated with blue cushioned chairs and it was elegant and huge. As he travelled on, he heard music and soon he noticed a man up ahead, seated on the hall floor, strumming on a ten-stringed instrument like a guitar. He did not fit in with the beautiful surroundings. He was dirty, grimy, dressed in tattered clothes, much as the man in the aforementioned dream.

Chris hardly paid attention to his words as he passed by, but he sang a tune. Later, as he was further down the hallway, Chris recalled that he had sung to him, "Why don't you come with me and I will show you the wonders of Padaran!" Chris was approaching a corner and he felt as if he would find glory and splendor in his view when he turned the corner, like the gates of Heaven. The dream ended with him at this point.

Chris pondered this dream for a long while and it took on an important meaning for him. The key to unlocking this dream was to realize that the guitar player with the decrepit look was representative of his ego self, his old nature. It is significant that Chris attached great value to his musical career, at times seeking freedom in his guitar playing. At the time he was overly attached to it.

Trying to find Chris' friend in the dream represents trying to find the way of thinking that he represented. This way of thinking is a philosophy that says happiness is found by doing things, by travelling, experiencing activities and looking for happenings that are exciting. Chris spent a good part of his life as a young adult living by this way of thinking, looking to find himself by experiencing things external to himself. This way of thinking and living was leading him into the "dirty subway" of the dream that represents a low level of spiritual awareness, unkempt and messy like the subway in the dream. As the dream underwent a change to more beautiful surroundings, Chris was also changing within himself. Rather than looking to external experiences to fulfill his life (which is a form of running away from yourself), he was looking inside through the help of dreams and other spiritual practices to find who he was in truth and to become aware of those traits and ways of thinking that were foreign, not a part of his true nature.

This is the point where the guitar player in the dream is so significant. As we have mentioned, the key to happiness and growth as a person lies in discovering yourself, in learning about the ego self (represented by the guitar man), so that you can free yourself from those old, undesirable ways of thinking that are holding you back.

Let us move to the significance of what the man was singing, "Why don't you come with me and I will show you the wonders of Padaran?" While working on the original manuscript for this book as a young couple, we lived in a motel, then later an apartment in town, across the street from Delaware Valley Community College. We would go to the college library to find a quiet place to work on the book. One day we came across a book called **From Egypt to Canaan** by John Ritchie, and became engrossed in the story of how the biblical journey of the children of Israel from Egypt through the desert to the Promised Land was a metaphor for the journey everyone undergoes as they leave behind the ego to find their true divine Self (the book expresses this journey in Christian terms).In the book it mentions a land called Padanaram, which lies directly outside the Promised Land. Over time we shortened that name to Padaran and adopted it as the umbrella name for many of the businesses we would become involved with.

Back to the dream, the guitar player was referring to the wonders of the land that lies just outside the Promised Land. Chris had reached that corner where a beautiful scene, just like the gates of Heaven, lay in store for him. The knowledge of his old nature, which dreams reveal to him on a daily basis, was helping him to grow to be the new creature that the Creator had created him to be, to be prepared to enter the Promised Land that was situated directly ahead. Thus, the guitar player, who represents his old self, holds the key to the knowledge of his new Self. The man who is being revealed to him is the one he can learn from to become a better man, molded by his true nature.

This process of growth has gone on inside him, mostly in an unconscious way as he has grown up and lived his life. The dreams have broadened his inner horizons immensely by helping him to be consciously aware of inner thoughts and feelings that were at one time unconscious or unrevealed. Ways of thinking that held him back or ruled his inner life are now revealed day by day in dreams, so that he can be aware of them and free from their limiting control.

We can walk through the process of inner spiritual growth as it goes on in a recurrent sequence of stages or plateaus.

In the first stage, you are in darkness, unaware that there is a problem or limitation that is pinning you down. It is quite possible to have a conscious existence and be unaware of the ramifications that your thoughts and actions are having in the unconscious realm of your existence. Have you ever met someone who complains a lot about the problems in their life only to realize that person is generally unaware of what they are bringing upon themselves?

In the second stage of awakening, you become aware of the problem that you have in your thinking, through a dream or inner revelation. However, you resist this awareness and fight against this truth because it makes you (your ego) look "bad." The ego, though illusory in its essence, has something of a life of its own, so it wants to remain hidden and work undetected, so it can be the "You" that is blindly going along in an unfulfilled conscious existence.

The third stage of awakening is where you have digested the awareness that has been revealed to you, have become willing to accept it and go about changing your life, changing your thinking, changing your actions. You see the wisdom of what has been revealed to you. This is called repentance in religious terms, but we do not want to attach guilt or blame here. When you change your thinking, you change your life, so we are affirming you are at the point of change. As you go through this process, the unconscious universe is reprogrammed through your ongoing change in thinking. A new reality is being created for you.

In the fourth and final stage, you have stepped beyond the problem that was revealed to you and it no longer has power over you. This problem no longer exists in your unconscious reality, so it no longer manifests in your conscious life.

The beauty of this process is that it is unique for you, fed from the unlimited fountain of your unconscious life guided by your spiritual nature, tailored to be understood by you. Based on that, the type of dreams you might have would be different from ours or from anyone else's dreams. Your mechanism for balance and harmony which is built into the dream process would be different from anyone else's.

You will see many examples of personal characteristics portrayed through people in your dreams. Depending on how you grew up, who were your relatives, who were the people you saw around you, who were your teachers, mentors, childhood friends, you will be molded in a certain way that will show up in your dreams. Also, whatever fears, hatreds, worries, anger, etc. that you might feel will be represented in those dream stories. It is all going to be welling up from that unconscious world that is running along simultaneously to the conscious life you are living.

What follows are some short examples of possible dream types and dream characters that you might encounter, based on our experiences with dreams. Of course, as mentioned before, yours will be different, but this can give you an idea of how things work.

Some dreams are instructional or even revelatory. The multidimensional character of dreams shows up in this one Chris had recently. In the dream, he was working on healing himself (in waking life he had some minor chest congestion). He was being shown how sound vibration can be used to heal; extremely specific sound frequencies can be used to heal specific conditions and drive away harmful viruses, bacteria, or parasites that cannot stand the resonance of that frequency. They become neutralized or downright destroyed by those frequencies. The dream voice was taking him through mathematical formulas, showing him out to six to eight decimal places how a specific frequency was useful to use against a certain condition. Not only harmful organisms, but also debilitating conditions, can be healed by the specific frequency. A number like 440.346895 frequency (just an example, Chris did not remember the exact number from the dream) could be used to heal a specific ailment. Then the dream voice continued, telling Chris to listen to the sound of the Holy Naad that was present throughout his audio awareness if he would be quiet and listen. (Another example of the Holy Naad is the cosmic sound of the Holy Spirit descending that Jesus' disciples heard in the Book of Acts). This is the sound like many rushing waters that people hear which is referred to throughout the Bible. The dream voice directed Chris that he could use this sound as a vibrational frequency to direct to various parts of his body for healing. In the dream Chris was directing the sound to his third eye, to his throat chakra, then to his heart and to his root chakra. When the sound would slip away, it was because he was getting caught up in his thoughts, but if he quieted his mind, the sound would come back and he could direct it again. The dream voice indicated that this is a "full spectrum" healing sound that is useful for healing all conditions.

    Chris woke up pretty much in awe of this dream. On one level, the symbolism could be seen to represent his efforts at healing himself from the chest congestion. But on another level, he was being instructed in a deep metaphysical truth. He was being shown methods of healing that humanity is just beginning to scratch the surface of in its consciousness. Chris was reminded that the dental assistant had cleaned his teeth several weeks back with a sonic device designed to kill the harmful bacteria at the gumline. And years earlier, when they had a problem with rats in the attic, they had purchased a sonic device which drove the rats away with a specific high-pitched frequency outside the frequency of human hearing.

    Daya, being a healer, was aware of Fibonacci healing, which uses a specific frequency for healing. She had mentioned it to Chris, but he was not fully aware of the details. After this dream, he made up his mind to study sound frequency healing and how it can be used. He is thinking that humanity will discover the frequencies that work for specific conditions and these will become one of the mainstream methods of healing. The Holy Naad, the sound of OM and various root sounds carry tremendous power to heal. Intuitive science will discover the specific frequencies that will resonate the body into healing from specific conditions.

Whereas the principles of spiritual healing through frequency are a type of spiritual truth, another kind of dream might be showing you religious characters who are less sincere about their commitment to spiritual truth and more attached to dogma, unbending in their view. Our dreams have shown us religious characters, eastern and western, in religious settings of all kinds talking about religious ideas and being attached to them or hypocritical about them. There is a difference between spiritual truth and false religion, between being real and phony. These dreams are pointing you away from the insincere religious wanderings of the mind to the truth of your being.

Another example of dreams that are showing you the ego-driven personality might involve famous celebrities appearing, such as musicians, actors, politicians or sports heroes. In these dreams, you see characters and settings where you are imagining being a star, being addicted to the famous musician's or celebrity life. Along with this is anxiety and fear of success simultaneously bundled in. These dreams are revealing these crushing ego driven forces that are driving you. Being aware of them, you can choose to step away and just be.

At other times you might see someone tempting you in a dream. If you are being enticed by someone in a dream it represents a way of thinking that is "invading" your consciousness and trying to draw you to that certain way of thinking. This could be through force (generally male) or coercion (generally female). Dreams can be graphic, but don't generally represent a literal understanding of the events portrayed. When you have one of these dreams, search through the recent past or make sure you are aware of inner events in the near future. What way of thinking was (is) drawing you in?

Your mind can be used by your ego to try to rule your true Self. This will show in your dreams when it happens. We met a wise man we called Smitty when we lived in Philadelphia (more on this later). One day, we were walking near City Hall and he pointed to a statue, built onto the upper façade of the building. His gesture told Chris he meant "look and study". Chris looked up and saw a statue with two figures.

One was a woman, facing the west, with a book in her lap. She was writing in the book. With his back to her, facing the east, was a man deep in thought. Smitty said nothing but he kept gesturing and motioning to Chris. It was slow to dawn on Chris that there was something being shown to him by this statue that was important for him to know. He pondered and prayed and finally figured it out. On the one hand was the woman, who represented book knowledge, the type of understanding that comes through the intellect and through words. On the other side was a different kind of knowledge, one that comes from deep thought, meditation and being in touch with one's own Self. This is an example from an actual conscious experience, but it is similar to the message in many dreams that reveal the difference between intellectual understanding versus knowing. Chris had been brought up in a highly intellectualized environment but needed to shift his focus from being ruled by his intellect. He needed to focus more on inner knowing.

At this point in his life, Chris was grappling in his inner life with what truly constitutes wisdom and understanding. His friends and buddies jokingly chided him by calling him "Harvard" all the time. They were unimpressed by his book knowledge, his intellect and what they saw as his "know-it-all" attitude. They were aware on some level of a different wisdom, which cannot be fully learned in books, but only comes through knowing your own heart and spirit. This is an awareness of things as they truly are, things beyond the surface, gained through experience, that is much akin to what is called "street" knowledge. It is a knowledge of the truth that words can help to guide you toward but can never fully reveal for you. We forget that words have always been a pointer to things and never the thing itself. Only by sincerely seeking to know, experiencing, can you truly come to real awareness and wisdom.

In Chris' dream life, he went through a period where dream characters appeared, who represented this overly intellectual approach to life, an overactive mind that is never quiet, always trapped in thought but never allowed to truly "Be". We called them the "Harvard" spirits since they became such a regular character in dreams at the time. They might be college students, professors, debaters, politicians who love words, or just people who argue back and forth in the dream. They are aspects of the ego that are hung up on intellectualism but not content in the bedrock of understanding. The ego loves to be "right" but does not know how to be truly happy. Look at your cable TV "news" station any day in America and you will see egos loving to argue, debate and prove their intellectual position. The ego lives in a world of duality, not harmony. Your deeper Self does not bow down to your intellect but only sees it as an aspect of your personality that can be used for good (or not).

Blare Magazine

Daya had a dream in which she was on the cover of a magazine, called "Blare Magazine", along with her mother and her aunt. Her aunt, who was her mother's sister, had aspects of her personality that were accusatory, vitriolic and bossy on the outside, who often had a jaded outlook on life. Daya's mother had struggled hard to raise her three children and she always had a contentious relationship with her sister. As we analyzed the dream, we came to see the magazine representing our dreams as we recorded them in dream journals, which typically "blare" the inner news of the day. The characters on the cover were aspects of a situation that was troubling Daya, symbolized by the contention that existed between her mother and sister and how that was playing out in her inner life. The word "blare" is also significant in the way that ego can be loud, squawking, accusatory, as it was in the inner incident portrayed in the dream.

Smitty

When you are open to it, there are times when it becomes clear that there is more to this world than meets the eye. There is a magical, mystical quality to life that is often overlooked in the crush of the concerns of daily living. When you step outside of those concerns by slowing down, tuning into the Divine flow, you open to seeing this magical, mystical existence. This happened to us in a strange way when we first met as street musicians playing music on the streets of Philadelphia. There was a liberating quality to our daily living, because we did not have regular jobs or a set schedule or sometimes even a place to live. We had no bills to pay, no obligations, no concerns except making it through the day with the basics of living.

The work of our life was spiritual growth; we spent our downtime from musical performance talking about dreams, yoga, metaphysical truth and getting to know each other. Things began to happen while we were thus engaged, things that you cannot really explain in a logical sense but only make sense if you acknowledge that there is a deeper reality at work beyond the surface world.

Chris vividly remembers something that happened just prior to the time that he first met Daya. He had met a group of people who did a regular Bible study and they invited him to come to the building where they were meeting. He had gone to a few meetings and began to get a crush on one of the women at the meeting. He was dimly aware that she was more interested in the minister than him but held out hope that he might be able to obtain her interest. After one of the meetings, the whole group took off for a walk through the busy streets of Philadelphia. As they walked across the plaza at City Hall there were people moving around them in all directions. Chris' "love" interest was walking ahead of him next to the minister. Out of nowhere from his side, a man walked up to him and started walking alongside him. Chris had never seen him before. The man was short and had the appearance of a homeless person or possibly an alcoholic with unkempt clothes and a ragged look to him. As he walked by, he spoke to Chris and said, "She is not for you (pointing to the woman in front of him); she's not interested in you and she likes the minister, so you need to move on from her". As quickly as he came, he kept moving on and was gone.

Chris was stunned on several levels. Firstly, how could this anonymous man know about what was going on in his mental/emotional space? Chris' ego was miffed about the message he delivered, but it clearly was a message and he was a messenger. Was he an angel? To this day, Chris does not have a logical explanation but that certainly made him think about that possibility. It was clear he needed to move on from that young lady and eventually the Bible study group, which helped to set the stage for some more miraculous occurrences in his life.

Dreams Can Change Your Life

At the time, Chris was living as a young man in Central Philadelphia in a low-end hotel that was soon to be condemned because of its' poor condition. One day he was trying to go to sleep and he was being kept awake by loud noises coming from a room one floor above across the courtyard outside his window. There was loud talking of two men and occasionally, an object would come flying out the window and crash in the littered courtyard below. This was not the first time this had been going on and Chris was fed up with it. He decided to head over and confront whoever was making the noise. That is when he met Smitty.

Chris knocked on Smitty's door and heard a gruff, scratchy voice that welcomed him in. Seated in the room, that was overwhelmingly cluttered, was Smitty and his friend John, though it was hard to pick them out in the dimly lit room with all the stuff scattered throughout. Smitty was an extremely black man who was seated in an armchair by the window. The light filtering in from the window behind and to the left of the chair was significantly brighter than the surrounding room, making it next to impossible to see Smitty, or to pick him out from the surrounding patchwork of clothes and furniture. His friend John was seated in a chair nearer to the door on the right, sitting perpendicular to Smitty in his chair. His proximity to the door and distance from the window made it easier to see him. As I found out later, John was a working man who came by to visit Smitty on a regular basis.

You had to work to understand Smitty as he spoke, much like you had to work to see him mixed in with his surroundings. He had a gravelly, muffled voice that Chris later found out was from a throat injury. But Chris soon figured out that he was welcoming him in and offering him a chair, which he had to isolate and separate from the clothes strewn across it. Chris spoke his peace about the bottles he was tossing from the window and Smitty apologized, but somehow Chris' anger had dissipated already. This place was so different from anyplace he had ever been, but somehow, he felt strangely at peace despite the cluttered surroundings. They spent the next few hours talking, mostly Smitty talking and asking Chris questions about himself. John and Smitty occasionally sipped from wine bottles sitting on the floor, but Chris refused the offer of a sip. He walked away from that meeting strangely elevated, feeling more in touch with himself, but bewildered in a way that he could have gained anything from an encounter in such an environment.

It became a regular event for Chris to meet Smitty either on purpose or coincidently. There was a connection there that is hard to describe, as Smitty became like the proverbial Zen master doing all sorts of outrageous things to goad his student into understanding. Smitty never held back in shattering Chris' dearly held ego delusions. He had sized him up quickly and did not hold back in crushing his intellectualism, naivete, pride and lack of understanding. Although blunt, this was never mean, and there was an underlying love between the two. Chris had a sincere desire to know the truth. It was clear that the Universe had provided an unconventional ally in Smitty to help him get to that place.

Smitty played a key role in joining us together, as excerpted from Daya's book **The Only Way Out Is In**. "Chris and I shared the same bed. We loved each other but we both decided we did not want to be intimate unless it was God's will. So, as we did and still do, we prayed for God to show us in no uncertain terms what we were to do. We asked for a sign.

While lying next to each other in that bed on the floor, we prayed. It was the first of July. We asked to be shown within 30 days His Will for our relationship. We promised that we would not be intimate until we heard what His answer was.

On July 31, 1979, we were in Fairmount Park. There was no one around or near us. We were laughing, talking and enjoying ourselves together.

The next thing we knew, as we were sitting on a bench, was Smitty coming along and walking towards us. He was smiling with his eyes twinkling like stars in the night sky even though it was broad daylight.

We got up to greet him with hugs. He sat down on the bench and we stood in front of him. He grabbed Chris' right hand and my left hand and was gently talking with us very casually.

Then he asked Chris if he felt he was a lucky man to know me. Chris said, 'Yes.' He asked me the same question about Chris. I said, 'Yes.' He then said, 'Whosoever God has joined together let no man put asunder. You are now husband and wife.'

Dreams Can Change Your Life

Stunned! We both briefly wondered what just happened. Our prayer, we recognized, was just answered as casually as that on the 30th day.

There was no big fanfare, no church, no bridal gown, no organ playing, no bridesmaids, best man or other traditional trimmings. But we were just as happy as if it had been that way. We hugged and we kissed. There was no question in our minds that God had spoken and we were now joined.

Our prayer was not pre-packaged in a response to fit our ego needs. If it had been, we would not have been aware of it being answered in the way it was. We just wanted to know God's will for us and Smitty was acting as his angel and our holy witness. And it was so.

Smitty said to Chris, "You will need to tell Daya, 'I Love You' every day. Don't ever forget to remind her how you feel." Chris agreed that he would do so and he has done that for the whole time of our relationship together.

Smitty had a sister who lived in North Philadelphia who worked in the medical industry. We visited her one Sunday along with Smitty and had lunch together. Smitty later had a stroke and his condition worsened. I think her connections helped to land him in a convalescent center in Center City. We visited Smitty there several times. One time we went to visit him where we had before; he was nowhere to be found, but eventually we found he had been moved to a different floor in the facility, so we met him and talked to him there. We moved out of the Philadelphia area, but we continued to look in on Smitty whenever we were back in town visiting Daya's relatives. His name was James Smith. On one of our visits to Philly, we stopped by the convalescent center to visit him. Once again, he was not found in the usual spot, so we went back to the front desk to ask them to trace down the location for James Smith. The man looked through the logs of all the patients who had been at the facility, at present and in the past. There was no James Smith on record. We explained that we had visited him many times in that building. He looked again. He could not find his name anywhere. That was that, as if he vanished into the ethers. We never saw Smitty again and never could explain what happened to him or why there was no record of him at that facility. We thought of tracking down his sister but did not recall her full name or address. We remain baffled about what could have happened.

So, what does this all have to do with dreams? It's just to point out that it is time to look beyond the surface of things, beyond your conditioned reality, beyond your comfort zone of expected behavior to realize that there is a profound reality at work beneath the surface of all things. Once you become open to this reality, it will begin to reveal itself to you. Once you place your feet on the path to understanding the deeper truth, things will happen in your life to guide you along the way. Your dreams are one of those steppingstones to open to this reality. They come from an awareness that resides in that unfathomable place. They unite the unconscious reality with your consciousness if you are willing to work with them. They show you how to "Be" your true Self by revealing how that true Self is looking at your daily inner life.

On the way to a realization, here is how the dream voice spoke to Chris. While sleeping and being unaware of what was to come the following day, he journeyed within to an imaginary place, echoing his former neighborhood in Enterprise, Florida. A group of residents in the area had a ritualistic habit, whereby after church on Sunday morning, they flocked to a local eatery, set in one of the older buildings found throughout this area. A voice was calling Chris to join them for this meal, but he felt the energy was stagnant there. He was determined to move on and he slowly walked/rode his bike/drove past this area down the street toward what he realized was his and Daya's second house up ahead; but he had forgotten they had this house, a familiar theme in many of his earlier dreams. In the previous dreams, the house was located on a large lot in the middle to several crossing roads in Somerville, Massachusetts. He had forgotten about the dream until he was driving with Daya the following day and saw a house under construction which looked a lot like the Enterprise house in the dream. It was a two-story modern box style, which are somewhat rare in Florida and used to be exceedingly rare.

Awake now, we went out for some food and brought it home for lunch, as is our custom lately when Chris works at home. We sat on the front porch on a warm sunny summer day but there was a beautiful breeze to keep it pleasant. We talked and ate. Chris was thinking about dreams, what an amazing journey they are. He spoke to Daya comparing the dream journey to the ancient 15th and 16th century explorers who set off to discover the world, how vast it was to them. We reflected how with dreams, we set off on a journey unbound by time and space to discover a vast universe that resides within.

We had worked on this manuscript for years, changing it and adding to it as we evolved. It was getting close to being complete, but Chris felt there was something missing, though he did not know what it was. He remembered recently being led to read some of the Canterbury tales, marveling at the way the stories were told and the way the language had a rhythm to it, not unlike a 14th century version of the way the best of modern day rapping poets attempt to tell their stories. As these thoughts melded together, he realized how they tied into the dream he had the night before. He was not content to settle for ordinary when it came to this book. He moved on from the ordinary and discovered that second house, which had been hidden from his memory. The words he had been looking for were there for us to build, under construction as it were; a rare but do-able work to be done. You are reading a sample of this blending now, concentrating on the current of ideas and language, flowing through the process whereby the stream of conscious life intersects with dream life to bring realization and revelation.

Why are the language and symbolism of dreams so strange instead of being direct?

Since we are coming from the perspective that the Divine Intelligence permeates all life, both seen and unseen; and that this loving energy moves toward harmony, balance, truth and peaceful happiness in all things (admitting free will in its conscious beings); then the dream process that happens at night is an extension of the work of this loving Divine intelligence playing out in the playground of your unconscious mind as you sleep.

We often asked ourselves, "why are dreams so non-sensical, or at the very least so very symbolic in nature?" We pondered this for a long while, for years even and then one day a small voice spoke to Chris, saying something like this:

"If you think about it for a minute, is your dream consciousness going to be contained inside the limitations of your three-dimensional world, inside language, inside the world as you think you know it? Is your dream consciousness limited to these boundaries of the ego mind? Is your dream consciousness even similarly confined to the conventions of your thinking mind? In reality, none of these things are true. You will find a closer affinity to your dream mind within your heart, within your feelings, but even then, it would not be limited to those or completely like those aspects of your being.

Think about a part of you that is aligned with infinite awareness, knowledge and understanding; a part that exists well beyond the boundaries of your physical dimension, well beyond the world that you have organized around your five senses, well beyond the rules of gravity, time and space. If you truly begin to understand how your dreams work, then you are beginning to get a glimpse of that deepest Self at work revealing you to yourself. You are beginning to see that radiant flash of infinite brilliance that you are in the 'present' and always will be forever. Each cell of your being, every atom in the Universe, intelligent energy that permeates all, is at work with your deepest consciousness, shedding light on who you are, revealing itself to you in your dreams so you can ascend the stairs of knowledge to meet the person you never left but might have forgotten for a time.

Imagine what it must be like for your Infinite Self to pry through the doors of the dark closet you have become within this planetary stage. How do you speak to a baby, or your cat in a way that they can understand? You would be trying to communicate but to them it might be gibberish. So strap on your best effort to understand, linking your thoughts and feelings to your will and charge ahead with reckless abandon to try and make some sense out of the seeming 'gibberish' that is coming in dreams to 'you' from 'You'; the one who is beyond time, space and limitation, the one who sees to the heart of things and is only trying to help you to do likewise."

Your mind is working through the immediate past or future to come to grips with what is going on in your inner world; in such a way that brings you to a state of balance, harmony, integration and making sense of it all; showing the path, enlightening, teaching, guiding. These are all functions of the "Holy Spirit", that inner enlightened part of you that blesses you with inner processes that help to discover the true "Self". By revealing what is going on with your inner life in unfettered fashion, your dreams reveal your true "Self" to the conscious you who might be too busily caught up in the distractions of daily living to notice. You do have to slow down, however, and tune in to that intuitive part of you in order to understand what the dream is saying.

    The forum where dreams gestate is the unconscious/subconscious mind, not the conscious mind of daily awareness. The rules of conscious life do not apply in the unconscious realm. This is not your logical mind that is used to the laws of conscious living where things follow certain rules of the physical universe. This is the unconscious realm where none of these rules apply and pretty much anything is possible if it relates to the emotional/mental context that the dream is presenting. In a recent dream, Chris saw a man in a standard car flying through the sky, doing loop-di-loops in the air in a show-off fashion, then slowly gliding down for a landing over our back yard and into the driveway next to our house (which, this being a dream, was not our "real" house but a smaller version whose yard we had been organizing). The furniture and plants we had been arranging in the back yard were miraculously moved against the fence in the matter of a few minutes when Chris returned from watching our son Joseph talking to the man who had just landed the car in the driveway. In this dream, we can see that the current known rules of conscious living do not apply here, a typical car of the day flying, furniture/plants being moved almost instantly or a logical sense of time being non-existent.

    The truth within the dream, or the logic of the dream if you will, is that it is consistent with the emotional/mental reality going on within your inner life during the time that the dream is revealing. Emotional response is equivalent whether real or imagined. For an analogy, Chris was riding his bike the other day; on the way home, he passed a group of Sandhill Cranes, large birds that walk the neighborhoods of Central Florida. He had no intention to harm them and generally they go about their business peaceably while he passes. Today, though, a large bird who was likely the leader of the flock, felt threatened and spread his wings and bellowed at Chris in a threatening defensive posture as he rode by. These birds, we assume, live their lives largely guided by unconscious, instinctual behavior. Though there was no real threat posed by Chris, something triggered inside this bird's mind to think that there was a threat and react accordingly. In a similar way, your inner unconscious interprets the mental/emotional flow of your life and reacts accordingly. Whether true, false or imagined, whatever you feed it will cause it to record and act as if it is real.

Imagine a situation where there was a strong sense of fear in an individual about a public speaking event. To the unconscious, this foreboding fear might be the same whether it was this speaking event, being nervous about an upcoming wedding, the first day of school, the first day of a new job, going to court, etc. The specifics of the event are not important in the unconscious realm, but the quality of the feelings and climate of thought create a mental/emotional package that feeds the unconscious. In this case, it would be a foreboding sense of the unknown. The unconscious is not bound by the logical, rational structures of conscious living. Things do not "make sense" in a dream because it is formed in a world where making sense in a rational way does not exist. You can fly in a dream. You can see fantastic creatures you never knew existed. You can move through time and space. The creative nature of your dreams is linked to your emotional life in a strong way, using imagery and a storyline to express those inner events but not bound to be direct about it. It is truthful in the context of your unconscious life but might make no sense to your conscious mind until you reach through and grab that link.

There is a tenuous link to your rational conscious mind in that you are aware of things happening in a dream, much as you are aware of your thoughts, emotions and the physical universe during conscious living. There is a "You" who is in the dream, either as a participant or an observer; but that is where the similarity ends, because the rules of conscious living do not exist in the realm of your dreams. For some reason, whether therapeutic, programmatic, purgative, or, as we believe for guidance, your mind creates these stories of emotional/mental events of the recent past or immediate future. They are a mirror reflecting back to you what is going on within you. Just as mystics of the past would stare into a mirror or pool of reflective water to receive guidance, get answers or see visions of events removed in time and space, so do dreams reflect back to you with an unbiased image of your inner life. They provide all the functions that the mystics were seeking, such as direction, inner vision, clarity, truth and insight.

The mythological and idiomatic language of the world bears similarity to dream language. We speak in idioms to explain universal truths. "A rolling stone gathers no moss" expresses the importance of moving forward with inertia to avoid stagnating in life. "Two heads are better than one" expresses how working together in cooperation can lead to improved results. "Curiosity killed the cat" warns that straying too much into areas that do not concern you can be counterproductive. "She is climbing the corporate ladder" talks to a person's ambitious job promotions. These are forms of symbolic language used to represent an inner truth.

Similarly, the mythology of the ancients and modern world use symbolic language to represent significant aspects of the inner life. The events that play out in our lives are represented in the stories of the gods, goddesses and heroes who populate the mythological stories. A lightning bolt from heaven could represent a moment of inspiration or a fiery tragic loss. Poseidon rising angrily from the sea foretells impending emotional upheaval where the vast depths of the sea represent the unconscious emotional/mental inner world. Even the superheroes of today's comic books and movies represent aspects of inner strength that we can call upon to meet the challenges of daily living.

As stated previously, the unconscious mind is closely aligned with the emotional body, not logical, rational or bound by the rules of conscious living. The eye of the soul pulls from the depths of this unconscious treasure trove to formulate your dream; to mirror to you the impact of the events of your daily living on your inner life. The emotional context of the dream is critical to understanding how to align it with the events of your conscious life.

Dreams Can Change Your Life

Chapter 6- Remembering Your Dreams

"And I went unto the angel, and said unto him, give me the little book. And he said unto me, Take it, and eat it up; and it shall make thy belly bitter, but it shall be in thy mouth sweet as honey."
Revelations Ch. 10 v 9

The process of remembering your dreams involves aligning with your subconscious/unconscious mind and tuning into your intuitive nature. These are two separate, but related, processes that allow you to remember your dreams in detail and to understand them once you remember the dream story. What good does it do to understand the theoretical underpinnings of what makes a dream if you do not remember any of your own dreams? In our years of working with dreams, this seems to be the number one roadblock we encounter when talking with folks about dreams and their tremendous value. Many people in our modern society are too busy, too occupied, too distracted to take the time to remember their dreams. We live in a world where immediate gratification, short sound bites and quick answers often seem to trump the value of slowing down and taking the time to find things of value. We are confident, though, that you, our reader, have made the decision that there are great benefits to slowing down and following the process to understand your dreams. Let us outline some steps you can take to help to remember and to understand your dreams.

First, we will talk about the process of remembering your dreams. We have outlined how these come from that unconscious, creative part of your mind. Unconscious mind is not logical, rational, bound by the normal rules of conscious living. It is more closely aligned with the emotional body so that the emotional context of the dream is critical to aligning it with conscious life. So how do you get in touch with this part of yourself? One primary key is to remember that you are generally most closely aligned with this part of yourself as you drift off to sleep or when you first wake up from sleep. It is important to use these times to align yourself with your dreams.

As you drift off to sleep, your mind slowly unwinds from the steady stream of conscious thought and gradually drifts through a process of winding down into different states of consciousness which can be correlated by measuring your brain waves. There are five of these consciousness states currently recognized, which flow into each other so there is not an exact border of demarcation between each of them. Beta is the normal waking consciousness. A deeper state of relaxation is the Alpha state, where you are closer to unconscious, aligned with your intuitive nature. Theta is the next level of light sleep, REM dream state which occurs as you leave the connection to consciousness and begin to sleep or conversely, when you are returning from the unconscious state at the end of your night's sleep. Delta is the slowest frequency where you are in a state of deep, "dreamless" sleep and present inside the unconscious, healing and renewing your system. Unrelated directly to dreaming, but possibly relevant to understanding your dreams is the Gamma state, the frequency at the high end of the Beta range where you are receiving insights and flashes of revelation.

Your job as a nascent dreamer is to create an environment where you can be present with the tools necessary to remember and record your dreams. You are going to pass from the unconscious to the conscious as you wake from sleep. It is during that time that the unconscious will pass over the dream story to the conscious mind in language and imagery that is understood by the conscious. If you take the time to be aware during that time, you can remember your dreams.

Remembering Your Dreams

You start by programming your mind as you go to sleep. Hold the thought that you are going to remember your dreams as you drift off to sleep. This will program your unconscious to act on this reality. In general, you want to hold onto thoughts of desired outcomes as you are going to sleep. You do not want to harbor negative thoughts, unforgiveness, resentment or fear as you drift off to sleep. Release those to the universe and replace them with positive visions of a reality you desire, forgiveness of perceived injustice, forgiveness of yourself and others and a courageous version of what you are capable of. Slow down your mind, focus on breathing and let go of the constant stream of ego babble. During this process, hold onto the message that you are open and receptive to remember your dreams.

Your unconscious will act on what you have told it to do when you awake from your sleep. You need to be ready. As we mentioned previously in our book, for years we kept dream journals in spiral notebooks which we kept by the bedside. We used a combination of words and pictures to record the dreams. Other people we have talked to find it easier to have a small recording device next to their bed so they can talk into it and record their dream when they wake up. Either way is fine; just find a method that works for you, that is simple and easy to act upon.

Write down or record whatever comes to you when you wake up. Make it a priority before the glare of the day's busy thoughts take over. Even small fragments are important. When you first start out you might remember only one small part of a dream. That small part that you write down can trigger a train of associations to reveal a larger dream, but either way, get it recorded. You are developing a process, training your mind, just like you might do under other circumstances of learning. Do not get frustrated if this does not happen right away. Follow the process and eventually it will work. The benefits are tremendous, so it is worth the effort.

Beyond dreaming, if you can focus on being more aware of your inner life as you go through daily living, this will help on many levels. When you encounter a significant event in your mental/emotional life, take time to note it to yourself. Don't let it pass by unnoticed. Apart from helping with your dream life, this has the added benefit of helping you to take control of your life by being aware of your thoughts and emotions. There is a process involved here as well. You are pulling back from being defined as your ego to a place where you are in touch with your higher Self. Typically, we humans tend to live our inner lives like a driverless carriage being pulled down the road by a runaway horse. Things happen; we react with thoughts and emotions without taking the time to reflect on what is going on. Imagine now that you are the driver of that carriage. You are going to determine the direction of your journey, how fast you are going to travel, when to stop and when to turn. You are going to work to become in control of your inner life. This will help with your dreams and in a larger sense, your well-being, as you live your live.

You have primed the pump by preparing your mind and your physical environment to remember your dreams. To help make your dreams more visual, if you keep a dream diary, you can draw stick figures or cartoons to represent the dream scenes, which will give further character and meaning to your dreams. Then you can write down the dreams as a story. It will enable you to focus on them and retain them long after you have written them down. You may want to jot down captions in the margins until you can fully write out what you saw happen in your dreams for that day. Do not ever feel your dreams are unimportant, too fragmentary, too embarrassing or judge yourself for what you see. Trust that your higher Self is revealing what you need to know.

If you awaken during the night but plan to go back to sleep, write down key words or key people so that you can remember the dream by morning. Pretty soon, all you will have to do is tell yourself what you are going to remember and it will happen. When you awake in the morning, lie still in bed with your eyes closed and review everything you saw. Do not get involved with chores first until you jot down your dreams. They will begin to fade and you'll forget important aspects if you do. Your remembrance will not get distorted if you record them right when you get out of bed.

Another useful technique is to review the day's events before you go to sleep. Think back on things that happened and your inner reaction to them. This is especially useful for making the link between what you see in a dream and how it relates to something in your inner life.

Do not give in to frustration, worry, fear or lack of believing as you seek to remember your dreams. Do not work too hard at it. Relax, follow the process, get in the flow and it will work out for you. Dreams are a gift from the unconscious realm. Belief requires no effort on your part, only the ability to receive. Inner turmoil and struggling stand in the way of remembering your dreams, like an electrical power grid might interfere with a car radio as you drive by it. If you forget your dreams, do not worry. The Holy Spirit knows what it is doing. It will cause you to remember what you should remember at the proper time.

Once you remember the dream, it is necessary to set aside some dedicated time to understand what it is about. As you become practiced at interpreting your dreams, understanding might come more quickly with some than others. Some might not make sense immediately, but the understanding hits you like a flash later in the day. We mentioned previously in this book about the three keys of dream interpretation; that being generally a mind that is focused and concentrated, open to listen to the intuitive voice; using whatever can be understood in the dream to start the process of unravelling the symbolism and meaning.

If you have developed your inward focus, the mental/emotional events in your daily living will not be passing by disregarded, but chances are good you will be more aware of them. It is beneficial, like the patients on Freud's legendary couch, to talk over your dreams with someone, a dream partner if you will. Tell your dreams to this person and they can ask you questions about the dream. Your dream partner can tune in to their intuitive nature (as you also are doing) to see what comes out of the dream story. You want to find out the impact of the various components of the dream.

How did it make you feel? What is the mood of the dream and what emotions does it bring up for you?

What does a particular event or character in the dream mean to you? Work to understand the symbolism as it applies to the dreamer.

What has the dreamer been going through recently in their mental/emotional life or what is anticipated for the day that lies ahead?

Remembering Your Dreams

Focus within. What parts of your inner life are coming forth in the dream? How does the dream story mimic a storyline happening in your inner life?

In our life together, we have talked over our dreams on a daily basis. As an example, this morning, Chris had the following dream which we discussed:

"I was trying to go to our old church service, which was in a different building, an older yellow wooden building. I was inside trying to get to the second floor where the service was held but the stairs began eight feet off the floor. Someone had piled a bunch of paper, newspapers, magazines, envelopes, all kinds of paper to make a stack to try to get to the stairs, but it fell over. I was picking up the paper to make two stacks to try to walk up to the stairs. I noticed an older couple was standing behind me watching me work. Then my focus shifted to an elevator in the lobby over to the left, where I saw some people getting ready to go up to the second floor."

We talked about this one and Chris realized he was doing a lot of mental and physical busywork, paperwork if you will, to try to fix things with Daya's medical insurance and medical appointments coming up, which seemed to be an obstacle in his mind. In reality, everything was working out exactly as it should without his intervention needed. Using the elevator symbolized his dawning awareness that there was an easy way for this to work out. The goals of healing and a proper mindset were aptly symbolized by the former churches service, where these goals were primary emphases.

On the same day, Daya had a dream where she was trying to call Chris to help her but was using the name of her ex-husband, who was intimidating her to do what he wanted. She was paralyzed from speaking though and the words were not coming out, so Chris was not responding. When he did not answer, she became frustrated.

Chris asked Daya if she felt oppressed recently and she recalled last night during a phone call. A medical office had called and left a message regarding some new equipment they were recommending being delivered to her. She called the office. While speaking with the man, he asked if she was using oxygen currently in relation to the new equipment they were recommending. Chris made a motion to indicate that she respond no to that question since he felt they were not referring to the cans of oxygen she had purchased on her own, but rather were asking whether she was using a medical oxygen breathing apparatus. Daya thought he was telling her not to accept the medical equipment they were recommending. This frustrated her because she was agreeing to accept the equipment. She saw Chris's actions as similar to the intimidating behavior of her ex-husband trying to force her to do something she did not want to do. Because she was a phone call with another person, she could not communicate with Chris to understand what he was saying, so she thought he was telling her not to accept the equipment. This led to the feelings of being bullied and frustrated, but unable to communicate and clarify in the current circumstance of the phone call.

There are analogies with working on a jigsaw puzzle when trying to understand your dreams. With a jigsaw puzzle you might have an image of the overall picture, or maybe no picture at all to work from. You start by putting together the pieces that fit with each other. As you do this, sections of puzzle pieces come together and you might see a linkage how one section can fit with another. You stumble along the way and find that sometimes the pieces you thought fit together actually do not, when you get a sense of the larger picture. Eventually, all the pieces come together, everything matches up and you get the whole picture.

Your spiritual mind working through the unconscious puts together such a masterpiece each night with your dreams. Each piece of the story fits together to tell the tale of your inner life. Your dream might have sections like the sections in the jigsaw puzzle. Chris was building a paper stairway of frazzled thoughts to try to get to a clarity regarding the medical insurance situation in the dream mentioned above. In the dream story, he was putting together the two stacks of paper to reach to the stairway sitting eight feet off the floor. This is the first section of the dream that he was able to comprehend by linking it to his mental (and physical) activity the night before and morning after the dream. His unconscious "recorded" the mental/emotional turmoil that was going on regarding the insurance situation as a root level uneasiness, frustration and restless energy. It then fed this root level feeling back to the conscious mind, when he was waking up, as this section of the dream story; translating it, if you will, through the Higher Mind, from the "language" of the unconscious to the language of the conscious mind. Chris used his intuitive faculty to link back from his conscious mind to what the unconscious was revealing in the dream story.

The people lining up to take the elevator to the second floor were a seemingly insignificant element of the dream. They might be considered as another section of the jigsaw puzzle of the dream story. In this section, however, a key was provided to the solution for overcoming the mental/emotional unease that Chris was experiencing. Generic people often represent a series of thoughts in dreams. In this case, a series of thoughts around the idea that there is an easier way to get to the second-floor church service, or to achieve clarity about the medical insurance situation. There already was an automatic process in the works where the professionals who work at the doctor's offices were communicating with the insurance company to work out all the details of the appointments and coverage. This automated process was symbolized by the elevator, which gets the job done even though you may not fully understand it or do the work yourself to make it happen.

Another section of the puzzle involves the couple standing behind observing Chris working on putting together the stacks of paper. A balanced male/female couple observing the situation who happened to be older could represent an integrated higher wisdom working within Chris to resolve his mental/emotional turmoil and point him in the direction of a solution that would bring peace and clarity. After the couple appeared in the dream, Chris shifted his focus over to the elevator, which provided a new perspective that what he was so energetically working towards on his own was already happening with no intervention on his part.

Section by section, your intuitive Self puts together the pieces and sections of the dream story. We have outlined how you can program your unconscious mind to help you to remember your dreams. You are becoming aware of your inner life as you go through daily living, taking time to reflect on what you are experiencing in your mental/emotional world. You are going to setup an environment that is conducive to working with your dreams as you drift off to sleep and wake up after sleeping. Take the time to find out which methods work best for you. Be still and quiet when you awake and record whatever elements of the dreams that you remember. Remain in this stillness or get with a dream partner to discuss the dreams once you have recorded them. Tune in to your intuitive Self to work through each element of the dream story and make the connection of how it relates to your inner life. As you go through this process you will experience the harmonizing, balanced realization, guidance and inner growth that your dream life provides as a gift from your Self to yourself.

Remembering Your Dreams

Chapter 7- Types of Dreams

"Once upon a time, I dreamt I was a butterfly, fluttering hither and thither, to all intents and purposes a butterfly. I was conscious only of my happiness as a butterfly, unaware that I was myself. Soon I awaked, and there I was, veritably myself again. Now I do not know whether I was then a man dreaming I was a butterfly, or whether I am now a butterfly, dreaming I am a man."
   Zhuangzi, The Butterfly as Companion: Meditations on the First Three Chapters of the Chuang-Tzu

Dreams can be understood on many levels. There can be an aspect that relates directly to this three-dimensional material world, such as when you dream that you are late for work and wake up to find out that your alarm clock did not go off as expected. Dreams invariably have the aspect that relates to the story about your mental-emotional inner life in what is essentially present time. Beyond that, dreams can be lucid, creative/problem solving, prophetic, recurring, or nightmarish. Let us explore some of these different aspects of some dreams.

Lucid Dreams

Many people report having dreams described as "lucid" dreams, which is a term used to describe a dream in which you are consciously aware while you are dreaming. You are aware of your thoughts and emotions much like you would be during waking life. In so-called regular dreaming, you might be an observer to the events or experiencing the events much like in a movie, but in lucid dreaming, you take it up a notch, in that you are conscious and know that you are dreaming. We have experienced this on rare occasions and it is a powerful event.

Over time a school of thought has developed around lucid dreaming, seeking to induce lucid dreaming and use that conscious awareness attained during the dream to control the flow of the dream. The thought is that by controlling the dream, you can learn to control inner complexes being presented in the dream. For example, if you are having a dream where you are being attacked by a tiger, you might choose to confront the tiger and chase it away in the lucid dream. Assuming the dream was representative of a fear you had, your confrontation of the tiger would help your ability to control and release that fear in waking life. There is a long, oft debated, history of how these ideas of lucid dreaming came about, which is not a subject we will discuss here, but advise the reader to research on your own if you are interested.

We do not want you to lose sight of a dominant feature of dreams, that they reveal your inner life to you, by becoming obsessed with inducing lucid dreaming. Since your dreams reveal to you that which is transpiring in your inner life, transferring those lessons to conscious living is one of their main benefits. Dreams can be instructive in becoming aware of the hang-ups that drive you, taking charge of your thoughts and working with your emotions in a balanced way to achieve harmony and equanimity in your life. As you do this, your dreams will reflect the changes you have implemented in your daily living, since the life of your unconscious mind responds directly to the dominant thoughts and feelings of your conscious daily living.

Types Of Dreams

Conversely, that which is programmed in your unconscious mind tends to gestate your responses to your life in conscious living. New-thought people and sports psychologists are aware of the practice of reprogramming the unconscious in order to initiate a desired result. When you take control in a lucid dream, in effect you may be reprogramming your unconscious in a different direction. It has been shown through experimentation, as mentioned before with recurring nightmares, that training people to take control during the nightmare can help to alleviate them or make them disappear altogether. Thus, this exercise in control helps to change the underlying phobia or fear that was causing the nightmare. Another benefit of lucid dreams is in the reprogramming of motor skills. Re-enacting an activity during a lucid dream reprograms the neural pathways, comparable to practicing that activity in conscious life.

During the process of studying your dreams and gaining meaning from them, you are in a way, waking from a dream. You are being "born again", pulling away from identifying with your ego self and becoming one with your higher Self. This is the predominant benefit of working with your dreams, since they reveal to you daily that which is important to the real You. Like peeling back the layers of an onion, you become aware of different limiting thoughts and feelings that are holding you back. You also become aware of the moments of ascension, thus ascertaining what joy, peace and blissful happiness are meant to exist in the childlike simplicity of your divine nature. This is the real work of dreaming and to the extent that lucid dreaming can help in this process, it can be useful; but it can become a sideshow if not kept in the proper perspective. It can be a bit of putting the cart before the horse, so to speak, if you become too focused on seeking to have control during lucid dreams rather than learning from all your dreams to initiate change in your conscious living. Though true that the unconscious life impacts your inner responses to daily living, your conscious intent to change will in turn modify that unconscious programming. It is a bit like the old conundrum of which came first the chicken or the egg, but it will take conscious intent to ascend the pathway to your true Self. Because of this, you want to be aware of your thoughts and emotions as you live your daily life. If you happen to gain that ability during certain lucid dreams, it can be helpful.

Creative Dreams

Creative people find answers and ideas, using their awareness during a dream, to find solutions and inspiration they are seeking. Movie director James Cameron developed his first glimpse of the Terminator in a fever induced dream. James Watson, co-discover of the structure of DNA, was inspired by his dream of a spiral staircase to envision the double helix structure of DNA. A famous creative inspiration occurred in the poem **Kubla Khan: or A Vision in a Dream,** by Samuel Taylor Coleridge. Coleridge writes in his preface how the poem was inspired by an opium induced dream and he woke to record the words that came to him in the dream, until he was interrupted, thus rendering the poem incomplete.

Daya, who is also a musician who plays the guitar, learned the chords to several songs in different dreams that she has had. She described one like this: "I was in a room and a man who had been a musician was teaching me the chords to a song. (I ended up writing the song after I woke up from the dream). He showed me the fingering of the chords which I had never seen before. It was a beautiful song." When Daya woke up, she showed the chords to Chris and he said, "Those are minor seventh chords; how did you learn to play those; I never saw you play them before?" She told him how she had just been shown them in the dream and the words came to her as well. We were both amazed.

At another time, Daya had a beautiful dream about a wedding in a gorgeous romantic island setting. It took place on the beach at night. The grooms were in a semi-circle around a campfire and the brides-to-be were in front of the campfire facing the grooms. On this tropical island, the brides were musicians. One of them had a crystalline necklace with graduated tubes hanging down that she played with her long fingernails. The longer tubes made lower sounds and the shorter tubes made higher sounds. One bride musician had a lap instrument shaped like an open wooden bowl that had metal strings across the opening that she plucked with her long fingernails. All the women had these sculptured long fingernails. A third bride had a lap drum made from wood with an animal skin surface. The women were playing a beautiful song by the campfire light, serenading their husbands to be. When Daya awoke, she remembered the song and put together the words, chords and melody to create a song that Chris and Daya perform until this day, called "Calm is the Night."

A recent creative dream that Chris had was stunningly relevant. The background to the dream involves the difficulties Chris was having coming up with a clear explanation in the prophetic dreams section which follows the current section of this book. He had also been contemplating the nature of his understanding of the Creator in the context of our modern-day scientific world. Here is the dream: "In the dream I was climbing, trying to reach the top of Mount Everest. I was in a steep valley trying to ascend near the top. I was climbing through the snow and there were rocks underneath at certain junctures with spaces between the rocks that made it very treacherous. I was having a difficult time and making little or no progress. At one point, I noticed off to the right there was a small window. I could see through the window an experienced guide who was leading tourists through a tunnel to the top of the mountain. I thought to myself 'That is not the real experience, but just a tourist version.' At some point later, a man appeared to join me. He was an experienced climber as well and he helped me to get through the valley to the top. A glorious path opened that went across a narrow crossing to the top of the mountain. It was a beautiful scene with bright sunlight, snowcapped mountains in the distance, clear skies and puffy clouds.

The scene switched to an area where there was smooth ice and blowing snow on the ground. Two men were standing on the ice, one of them with skates on. The skater was moving very tentatively on the ice, taking brief uncertain pushes forward with his skates. The other man told him he needed to be aggressive and bold with his skating if he wanted to convince the public. The other man took that advice to heart and skated off across the ice, sliding with a smooth, confident glide like an experienced skater.

Later, I was sitting in a lounge at the basecamp, looking through the picture windows to the outside. I focused in on a bug that was crawling on a tree stump. He was camouflaged to look like the bark. I noted how wondrous that was.

I remembered back to the top of Everest, thinking about how I arrived there and recalled a mode of transport that swooped down and brought me near the top. Another person nearby tells me, 'I'm sure you needed to take a vehicle from the bottom and work your way up to the top'. I pondered which of these views was correct, but understood somehow maybe they both were possible, as the dream ended."

The day before Chris had been working on the Prophetic Dreams section, struggling with concepts and wording around a new paradigm of consciousness and how prophetic dreams seem to defy the concept of linear time. This is represented by the part of the dream where he is struggling to climb near the top of Mount Everest, with the deep snows and rocky climbing representing the difficult finding clarity with the ideas and verbiage to describe them. Chris did a search online for some related terms and came across some information that was somewhat useful but not really getting to the heart of things. This can be seen in the dream with the scene at the window and the "tourist" version of the climb. He kept searching under the words "new consciousness" and found a real breakthrough, both with helping to clarify and explain what he was driving at. He came across information related to a new paradigm in consciousness that has its roots in theosophy, mysticism, transcendentalism, and new thought. He could see this is what he was driving at, being aware that a pure scientific study of dreams that ignores the enlightened consciousness that is involved cannot begin to fully understand their marvelous workings. This breakthrough in understanding is represented in the dream by the clear pathway that opens for the climbers at the top of the mountain.

A nod to the role of evolution and the theory of evolution, which appeared in the context of consciousness and science that Chris was exploring, appears in the dream with the camouflaged "bark bug". Evolution explains that those bugs who could survive in their surroundings by blending in were more likely to pass on their offspring to the next generation. Over time, this process developed a perfectly camouflaged bug. In the context of the dream, the role of creative "consciousness" cannot be overlooked in this whole progression, a consciousness that exists in varying forms to match at all levels of existence.

The skaters in the dream represent an inner transition in the clarity of presenting this material to readers of this book (the public, if you will). As first tentative and unsure, as represented by the skater, Chris had an inner conversation and gained clarity and surety to present what he wanted to say. He encouraged himself to not be timid about saying what he meant once he was clear about it.

The final section of the dream dwells on the role of inspiration coming from "above" and the role of the individual to work his way through to understanding and enlightenment. Both can exist together in harmony as you climb the mountain to illumination. Chris was seeing just that, as he worked his way through to clearly understand what he was driving at, while at the same time being lifted up by flashes of insight triggered by what he was studying and reading. On another level, the creative insight provided by this dream confirms the nature of the Creator, who exists "above" everything, as a consciousness that maintains an awareness of the All and sustains everything, while simultaneously existing within everything seen and unseen that is working its way up through all levels of existence. This awareness can "swoop down" into our awareness but also exists in every part of the participants and process as all creation evolves through to perfection. This consciousness pervades the universe at all levels, from the smallest sub-atomic particles to the largest galaxies, from the simplest of lifeforms to human experience, existing at a level appropriate to the existential situation. Understanding this dream clarified answers to these questions Chris had been pondering.

Prophetic Dreams

Prophetic dreams happen when you dream of an event which comes to fruition at a future time; or, in some cases you might receive a warning or message that relates to a future event. These are well documented throughout history. Julius Caesar's wife Calpurnia was warned in a dream that something terrible was about to happen. She tried to get Caesar to refrain from going out, but he ignored her and ended up going to the Senate where he was stabbed to death. King Xerxes of Persia invaded Greece after being moved to do so in a recurring dream. Ward Hill Lamont, a close confidant of Abraham Lincoln, writes of a dream which Lincoln had fourteen days prior to his assassination. In the dream that Lincoln shared with a small group three days prior to his death, he walks through several rooms hearing the sobs of mourners and comes to a room where there is a casket and asks a soldier guarding it who was killed in the White House. The soldier responds that the President was killed by an assassin.

In previous chapters, we explained how the dream stories about the inner life are essentially set in the present time, ranging from the day before to the day ahead. A large percentage of our dreams can be seen as prophetic, since they forecast the inner events that we are going to experience in the day ahead. The dream-maker is not bound by time and space, working with the unconscious which is similarly not even aware of the normal rules of life in the material world. When dreaming, you are tuned into a thread that can pull from the past or future.

Today Daya had a dream where Chris was trying to suffocate her with a pillow while she was sleeping on her stomach. She told Chris to stop and pressed back up to stop him. We talked about the dream in the car but could not make sense of it. A bit later in the drive Chris mentioned about how he wished he could burn the yard debris that he had cut down in the backyard. He had read more of the city charter (rules and regulations), which he had done before, and confirmed it was against the law to have an open burn like that. He explained to Daya that his definition of an open burn had changed. He complained about having to bag so much material for disposal. Daya responded that she wished he would stop bringing up this issue for the umpteenth time. We immediately saw the correlation of the emotional context of her feeling "suffocated" in the dream with dealing incessantly with Chris bringing up the trash burning issue numerous times.

Another element related to the prophetic nature of dreams is the experience you have when you are living through an experience and remember that you dreamt about it previously. Somewhat akin to a "déjà vu" experience, you see and feel in exacting detail that you previously dreamt about what is currently transpiring. We have both been through this event, feeling that either this represents what it appears to be, that you did actually dream of this previously in time; or, perhaps you have momentarily tuned into the timeless nature of reality, which to some part of your highest Self exists where all experience blends as one.

In either case, with prophetic dreams, you are certainly experiencing something that is exciting and marvelous. It is an area of fascination that indicates we are just beginning to scratch the surface of the true nature of our mind and reality. Working with your dreams plays with our concept of time. It is peeling you away from a process that links you only to those things associated with three-dimensional reality and rational thinking; tuning you into an awareness and tools such as intuition, sensitivity, insight, creativity and inspiration that are used to understand what you are experiencing. Think of it as being trapped inside a world that exists inside a giant glass bubble. Within that bubble there are certain laws and things behave in a predictable fashion. Outside the bubble exists an ever-expanding universe of possibilities. There are things going on outside the bubble that defy the rules that exist inside the bubble. When you begin to break through the glass that protects the bubble, you being to experience things that are hard to understand. You need a new paradigm to comprehend what you are experiencing.

Chris was reminded of a Mayan concept he read about some years ago. There is a model of our life in the world of time existing as a spiral circle moving upwards. As we move through the spiral, we come to places which exist on the same mathematical plane as spots on the lower levels of the spiral. We are presented with experiences which mirror the lessons we needed to learn at that lower level which we might have failed to master in the previous attempt. If we master that lesson in this attempt, we will no longer need to experience it again. If not, we will find the same opportunity being presented again when we reach the same spot on the next level of the spiral. Here is another way to look at the experiences of our inner life and how our dream life may tie into an understanding different than the concept of linear time we have become accustomed to.

Many people have tried to study dreams through scientific observation in the laboratory. Hopefully, they are beginning to see that this is a limited model capable of limited results which, although useful, cannot explain the whole picture. Prophetic dreams force us to consider the nature of consciousness and the nature of the reality we live in. They force us to confront layers of our mind and consciousness that seem to exist outside what we traditionally consider to be the laws of time and space. They help us to see there is a subjective nature to reality beyond the objective reality of our material life. Quantum physics bears out this observation at the smallest evident levels of the universe. At this level, conscious intention determines the objective reality that results. We are part of a universe unfolding through us; we are a consciousness capable of growing and learning from tools like our dreams to create a better reality for ourselves; one that is more in tune with our highest nature.

Recurring Dreams

Most of us have experienced recurring dreams; dreams that happen on multiple occasions where a recurring activity or theme takes place. Common recurring dreams involve subjects and themes such as going back to school, being late for something, flying, falling, being naked, losing something, being stuck where you cannot move. There are many possible themes to recurring dreams which will be unique to you and your inner life. Chris has had recurring dreams about being late for class many times which relates to anxiety he had around a perceived deadline or commitment. He also used to have dreams about bounding down the street he grew up on in giant leaps where he flew through the air for long periods of time. This related to feelings of elation around something he had accomplished around a core goal in his life, being empowered to make great progress forward. Recurring dreams can congregate around a certain period in your life, or they can span across the whole of your life, starting in childhood and recurring regularly throughout your life.

The dreams recur because they relate to a core issue or mental/emotional response in your life that keeps coming up regularly in your daily living. Chris' dreams about being late for class began with the reality that when he was in college, he was on a large campus and sometimes had to walk great distances from one class to another in a short period of time. It brought out feelings of frustration and stress about being tardy and facing the "shame" or embarrassment of walking in late to class; without really being able to control that outcome since this might have been the only time window to take that required class. There was an opportunity for growth being presented in the recurring dream. Over time, with the help of these dreams, Chris has begun to learn to not anticipate a particular outcome when his behavior could not keep up with his preconceived notions of what was acceptable. He learned to become more detached from results in these situations. There were situations where he could not live up to his expectations for himself, such as when he was late for a corporate meeting; if he didn't meet what he thought were the expectations of his boss or colleagues; or if he couldn't control the situation to meet all the outcomes he expected of himself. This recurring dream would come up regularly when he was dealing with these feelings of frustration, helplessness and anxiety about making it to a certain consequence. The dream content was not always exactly the same, but it involved walking across the campus trying to find his way and feeling the pressure of a deadline to make it to the destination on time.

    Recurring dreams relate to unresolved issues because those are the things that come up repeatedly in your inner life. We talked previously about the Mayan "spiral of time" concept and this can relate to recurring dreams. Those issues that you have not dealt with come up repeatedly as you pass through circumstances in your life which give you an opportunity to overcome and transcend them. The recurring dream could be happening at one of these "intersection" points where you are being presented with the opportunity to reveal the unresolved issue to yourself and take steps to move past it. These could relate to past abuses related to your family or bullying by other kids while you were in school. You could be a soldier reliving the trauma of the battlefield triggered by something in your inner life. Conflicts and disasters that were buried at the time could resurface in your recurring dreams; buried by stuffing your mental/emotional response in your unconscious so you could survive in the present moment during these events.

Types Of Dreams

These recurring dreams are great portals into self-discovery; a window into who you are and what issues you are facing, or what triumphs move the needle of your psyche. If you are having stressful or anxiety ridden recurrent dreams, you can use this opportunity to determine what is causing the stress and develop some positive actions to deal with it. No one will be immune from stress inducing situations in their daily life, but we can learn to develop techniques and methods to alter our perception of the event and respond in a balanced, harmonious way.

Positive affirmations are a great way to counter the stressful impact of situations. For example, if your recurring dreams relates to issues around lack of money, you can begin by affirming a positive affirmation, such as, "All my needs are being met by the universe and I am in the flow of prosperity and abundance." Repeat this or a similar affirmation to yourself at regular intervals. You may not believe it at first and you may initially resist the idea of stating this, but over time doing so will reprogram your subconscious mind and consequently alter the way you experience the world. An affirmation like this can become an anchor to toss into the sea of fearful emotions that might well up when you face an issue paying a bill or meeting a financial commitment. Eventually, this emotional storm will dwindle, and you will find ways to handle these financial situations.

Centering and quieting your mind are key techniques that can help you dealing with the "negative" issues presented in recurring dreams. Prayer is talking to God (however you perceive him/her) and meditation is listening to God. Both approaches are useful for overcoming mental/emotional struggles. Affirmative prayer states a desired objective with a positive statement to the Creator, universe, or however you speak to the center of your being. You are not pleading for something to happen but rather aligning yourself to the reality that it is happening (in the present). This has the effect to associate your inner mind with the solution rather than being stuck in the problem. A chain of constructive results follows as you line up with the creative power that underlies everything.

Meditation is the process of quieting your mind so you can harmonize your being and refresh your perception. You do not have to sit cross legged in a lotus posture but nothing against trying it that way. The key component is quieting the racing of your mind and detaching yourself from the constant chatter of your thoughts. Focusing on your breath is particularly useful when you are trying to meditate and quiet your mind. In fact, it is impossible to have a negative thought while you are focused on your breathing. You can visualize scenes like clouds gently passing by in the sky or the bubbling sounds of a mountain stream as it gently flows; this is not necessary as long as you learn to release thoughts that come up in your mind. Do not fight them, just release them and focus back in on your breath or whatever your focal point is.

Guided by your recurring dreams, these techniques can help you go within and discover ways to overcome the persistent challenges of your inner life. Perhaps you will begin to dream of flying or experiencing a beautiful vista in nature as you incorporate these changes.

Nightmares

Most everyone has experienced a nightmare, which is an intense dream that depicts a negative experience that can leave you feeling frightened, exhausted or abused. In a clinical medical sense, you wake up immediately after a nightmare dream, perhaps feeling terrified or sweating, but for our purposes you don't have to wake up immediately afterwards to experience the nightmare as we refer to it. You are being chased, attacked or powerless in the face of overwhelming obstacles in many of the nightmares that people experience. Nightmares are distinguished by the power of the experience and how bad you feel because of them.

Children experience nightmares in slightly higher percentages than adults, but these dreams can happen anytime in life. As you may have surmised from the major premises of our book, nightmares are reflecting to you when you are dealing with an intense mental/emotional climate of negative emotions in your life. This can relate to feelings of fear, anger, frustration, powerlessness or general anxiety. If you are consumed by these feelings, the nightmare will alert you to the intensity of what you are dealing with and hopefully serve as a beacon to help a process to set you back onto the path of harmony and balance in relation to these issues.

Our nightmares have dealt with a large range of scenarios; dreams can be starkly vivid and blunt as we have previously mentioned, presenting scenes that would be considered criminal, dangerous or socially unacceptable in waking life. Daya has experienced nightmares of attempted murder and rape, being attacked with various weapons and being chased in a car or on foot where she had to jump and climb over fences, trees and up buildings to escape. Chris has experienced nightmares where he was chased by wild animals such as bears and tigers, fighting ninja warriors and being present in the devastation of a war scene. Over time, we have seen that the issues presented in Daya's nightmares relate to her being attacked by a resistant mindset for taking a stand in her thinking about a certain situation. Chris' nightmares more often have dealt with issues of anger and frustration that he is confronting. The nightmare presents the inner dynamic going on with us as we experience these thoughts and feelings playing out in our inner life.

Occasional nightmares are common and we hope you will dig in and work with the dream imagery presented to gain an understanding of what you are dealing with. You can use techniques like those mentioned in the section on recurring dreams to step out of the negative emotions being presented in the dream. This process will lead to transcendence of the inner turmoil you are dealing with. If your nightmares are more regular and persistent, it is time to consider asking for help from a professional or someone in your life who can help you work through the issues that the nightmares are presenting. Oftentimes, if you identify and objectify the mental/emotional climate that led to the nightmare by identifying it through the help of these dreams, you have taken the first step of realizing that your true Self was never involved in this drama of your ego world. Next, you will take steps to change the way you perceive these issues in your conscious life. You will develop the tools you need to respond positively when confronted with strong emotions of fear or anger. No-one is exempt from experiencing these types of emotionally charged thought patterns, but we can develop techniques to reclaim our power when faced with these challenges in our inner life.

Chapter 8- Our Main Journey is the Journey Within

"For God speaks once, yea twice, yet man perceives it not. In a dream, in a vision of the night, when deep sleep falls upon men, in slumberings upon the bed; Then He opens the ears of men, and seals their instruction, that He may withdraw man from his purpose, and hide pride from man. He keeps back his soul from the pit and his life from perishing by the sword."
Job, Ch. 33 v 14-18

We have written our book with the premise that the foremost journey that truly matters is the inner journey, the quest that leads to Self-realization, "redemption" and the discovery of happiness within. We have shown how dreams come as food for the spirit that is seeking to know itself. They are like daily newspapers or news broadcasts on TV with information about the activities, personalities, thoughts, emotions and motivations of the individual's own inner life. As such, they help to strip away the mask of illusion and ego by which so many people are kept from discovering themselves as they truly are.

Dreams appear in a symbolic language of imagery and narratives that come from the Holy Spirit; they are meant to be understand by the same Holy Spirit working within us through intuitive understanding.

This dream language and understanding have the qualities of direct perception rather than being something of the intellect or "book knowledge". They are insightful, not rational.

Dreams are meant to guide us to the divine, joyful nature that lies easily available within us. Our own self is the desert through which we must wander to reach the Promised Land within. The experiences of our life are the means by which we are molded by the hand of God to discover the truth that lies within us. Dreams come to us as precious manna to feed our spirits on our daily inner journey, so we can continue to grow in awareness and knowledge of our Self and the truth of who we are. In this way, the light can shine through us and illumine the way for others, as many have done who have come before us.

Each person who grows up in this world becomes conditioned to ways of thinking and acting that work contrary to the best interests of our spiritual condition. For example, we adopt a certain religion, learn its way of thinking and viewing the world, only to find out that this religion that gave us such joy and happiness when we first embraced it has become the chain that binds our mind and spirit to a certain limited view of things, which keeps us from growing.

All of this acquired behavior and thinking is part of a conditioning process that defines in us an ego-self, a person who is limited, perhaps rigid and negative in his beliefs.

Dreams come to reverse this conditioning process and to break the shell of ego in which we are unknowingly encased. By revealing to us the naked truth about our inner life, those elements that contend against our spirit and try to stunt our growth are revealed to us, so that we can learn of our ego and how to guide and transcend it.

The following story is used to explain the process by which we grow spiritually through the knowledge revealed to us, perhaps overcoming resistance along the way. It is set during the time of the apartheid era in South Africa.

Chris was talking with one of the female students on the school bus that he used to drive. He had noticed that she had an English-speaking accent different than American, so he asked her if she was from England or Australia. She responded by saying, neither. She was from South

Africa; she had grown up there and moved to the United States a few years back.

As they talked, the conversation turned to the nature of the two societies she had lived in, South Africa and the United States. She commented that the United States was a much freer society. People in South Africa were liable to be thrown in jail for years without ever knowing what charge was being held against them. She commented that the people in South Africa were for the most part afraid; and they carried their fear around with them. This she noticed particularly when she went back and visited South Africa, which she did regularly.

Chris had asked her if there was much tension and hostility in the atmosphere of the country. They both agreed that this was probably due to the high level of oppression. It was here that she said something the clicked in Chris' memory. She commented how the people were afraid without even knowing they were afraid; and later she said, for the most part, the people who were oppressed were unaware they were being oppressed, since the oppressive conditions had existed for so long and become a way of life in the society. Likewise, the oppressors were similarly conditioned to a way of behavior that they considered proper, being oblivious to a different way.

When she spoke about conditions in South Africa, it triggered a memory in Chris about the time he had seen a black South African rugby team which was visiting the United States. The relationship between the white coaches and the black players showed that both the oppressor and those who were being oppressed were conditioned to exist along with the system they had inherited. Those Americans who were aware and used to the conceptual freedom of equality (though imperfect) seemed to be the only ones who noticed the oppressive conditions that existed in the relationships between the players and coaches on the rugby team.

This little story is used to exemplify the point that people exist in conditioned levels of awareness until something comes into their lives to awaken them to the nature of that conditioning and the make them aware of another way of thinking and behaving. Without this intervention, they are likely to continue in the conditioned view of life they have acquired. Each time the conditioning is revealed to the individual in such a way that this knowledge will free her from it, she is now able to grow to an increased level of awareness of herself and her world. If this process of revelation and freedom from conditioning is extended indefinitely, we come to the awareness of the Creator's Spirit, who is without any limits and who is aware of all things.

In the case of the South African rugby team, perhaps their experience with American society awakened some of them to the reality of their oppressive conditions; to the point where they began to grow to a greater awareness of what they would accept in their lives and what they would not accept from then on.

This process of breaking down limited conditioned behavior is one of the main benefits of dreams. Seen from the perspective of infinite awareness, dreams reveal the conditioning of your inner life as well as positive movements away from "dead" behavior. Like the members of the South African rugby team, chances are good that you are habituated by undesirable forces in yourself and in your interactions with people that limit you and your view of the world. Until you allow the *light* to be turned on these spiritual forces, you cannot be free from their effect on you.

You must un-learn the things that are binding you up, by focusing your attention away from the external world and looking at your internal world as the source of your problems. Dreams are healing tools capable of solving your problems by revealing the source of them, your inner conflicts and tensions that divide your mind and dissipate your energy. If you desire to be fully aware of the workings of your inner life, and to have an objective, truthful view of these workings, your dreams will give you this awareness, if you allow.

One of the new ideas that we have presented in this book is the realization that dreams are day-to-day messages concerned with the events of the recent past or immediate future of the dreamer's inner mental-emotional life (in other words, dreams are essentially about inner events of the present). As you read this book and re-evaluate things because of it, you may begin to have dreams that will represent the inner cleansing that is going on. This could be symbolized in a dream as taking a shower, going to the bathroom or shampooing your hair. You will become aware of things through dreams that were previously hidden from your awareness. This may seem troubling or confrontational at times, but the end result is that you are becoming aware of who you are in truth.

Inner growth will be depicted in your daily dreams as well as breaking free from the old nature that might have been chaining you down for a long time. You might see yourself in the middle of an arduous quest, battling with a relentless foe or confronting unsavory characters. Each situation will be unique to you, but your dreams will show you the inner characters of your personality and psyche that represent the old ways of thinking and reacting on a mental/emotional level. This is truly the work that each of us are called to do while on this earth, to release from the illusions that bind us and embrace our highest spiritual potential.

Picture if you will, the aforementioned South African rugby team and their coaches. If there was to be a change in the attitudes and actions of the members of that team, could it happen without a struggle? Most likely not. The ways of oppression are firmly entrenched, so that if the players were suddenly to see that their rights were being trampled on and demand a change, they would face tremendous resistance from the coaches and from the elements within themselves that have learned to thrive on the oppressive system. Likewise, if the coaches were to decide that they were too dominant over the lives of the players, there would be elements within themselves that would fight against their resolve to change their ways. Perhaps even some of the players would resist a change in the status of what they have become accustomed to. Sometimes you need a spark to ignite this type of change. As we saw in the history of South Africa, Nelson Mandela and the movement he represented became a spark that initiated great change in the country. Learning from your dreams can be the spark that ignites change within you. When you have that first dream lesson in self-discovery, it can be a high that carries you forward to greater plateaus of understanding.

You also may face resistance when you set out to change your life. Your dreams may show many inner struggles and confrontations with the forces that have been conditioned to a certain way of limited or negative thinking. You may have been at most dimly aware that this was going on inside of you. The naked truth is a shock to those elements of the ego that are conditioned to resist change for the good and happy to keep your "spirit" locked in invisible chains. Since dreams view things from the perspective of infinite awareness and complete freedom (detachment), they will reveal daily those elements that are holding you down from your God-given inheritance of freedom, life, love and happiness. The Holy Spirit (Divine Self) will never give up its work of revealing the truth to you, so that you can be free from adverse forces that keep you down.

We discover through our dreams that it is our way of thinking and feeling about the events of our lives that determines whether we have a constructive or undesirable experience on this earth. Dreams aid us by showing us the way we responded internally to a specific incident or a specific time in our lives. We can become aware of what is holding us back, as well as becoming aware of a more enlightened approach to a similar set of circumstances in our mental/emotional life. Time, in a spiritual sense, travels in a spiral where we revisit the same inner situations over and over as we pass by the same plane in the spiral of time, until we have learned the lesson that is needed. These intersecting moments may be related to the "deja vus" and recurring dreams that we experience. They keep coming back until things sink in, to the point where we have transformed within.

Chris had a dream that showed us that he was rushed, nervous, tense, impatient and heaping pressure on himself to achieve an imagined deadline while he and Daya were practicing music. This awareness from the dream made him see that if he had been relaxed, peaceful and patient during the practice session, without any imagined deadlines, the whole experience would have been different and enjoyable, both in the resulting dream and commensurate reality. While showing you what is going on with your inner life, dreams naturally point you to a better way.

Our habitual thoughts put us where we sincerely desire to be, based on the quality of those thoughts. This is true as it relates to our life with our family, friends, work, relationships, finances, opportunities and everything that goes on with us, within and without. If our thinking is limited, self-defeating or coming from a low energy level, it creates after its own kind, so we experience a mental/emotional life filled with self-defeating situations, never seeing beyond a limited set of opportunity and apparent negative situations. If we have thoughts filled with affirmation, confidence and optimism then we find solutions to the situations in our lives and opportunities for growth and happiness. Think of this reality as you live your life, as you react to circumstances in your life and as you look within at the quality of your daily thoughts. This process will unfold in your dreams as you become aware of the limiting factors in your thought life, confront them, change and begin to develop new, more life-affirming thoughts. Healing works from top to bottom and from within to without. Changing your thinking from top to bottom is manifested by bringing a higher level of consciousness into your thinking. Working from within to without plays out as you look inside, use tools like dreams to become aware of your inner life and change to a new paradigm in your mental/emotional life. This consequently affects the quality of your life in the external, "real" world.

Leave behind those things that are holding you back, whether it be in your thinking, your relationships, your finances, your habits or your work. Detach the strings that tie you down and do not be concerned how others feel about it. Here are some suggested activities to help you with this process:

List the things you have been accepting, even though you do not like or agree with them, from your thoughts, your relationships, your family, or your work life.

Make yourself bring up all the dregs before your eyes in black and white. Face it within yourself. Do not be afraid to admit to your conscious mind what your superconscious/subconscious already knows. It is important to discover your inner feelings, verbalize them by writing them down and saying them out loud. Then you can begin the process to release those ones that are no longer working for you.

Write down positive statements about the world you want to see, based on this previous list you have created. For example, if you do not like the way a relative has been speaking to you in a belittling manner, make a statement that this person is respectful and considerate in your dealings with them. Speak this statement out loud to impress it on your subconscious mind. If you believe it, the universe will take steps to make it happen for you. That relative might have an epiphany and change their behavior; you might be prompted in the moment to say something that makes them aware of how they have been treating you;

or, they might gradually phase out of your life. We have been taught to speak to the Higher Self of people who are intractable in their behavior to let that divine essence that exists in everyone work with them. Often, we cannot change others directly, but we can affirm the best for them.

Maybe, somewhere in some distant past humans lived closer to the animals, existing on the borders of the unconscious mind, responding constantly to the senses. Gradually, however, we "evolved" into the intellect and became a thought creature, caught up in the world of the mind. The recent past in the Western world and the age of reason and science might be the pinnacle of this way of being. Somewhere along the way we lost our connection with that deeper part of our intuitive nature that is not limited to the intellect but responds to feelings more intimately related to our emotions, gut feelings, messages rising out of the unseen. In today's world, there is a push to get back to our intuitive Self and the world is more ready for dreams, which have always been there to guide us.

We have been guided by dreams on our journey within and we hope you have enjoyed sharing that journey with us. Dreams can help to peel back the curtain of your soul so that you can realize your full potential as a human and divine being. First, you become aware of an ego self that is conditioned and limiting, but this awareness helps you to love and embrace that ego self without identifying with it as your dominant nature. You grow to discover a constant, immutable Self that works with you through your dreams, embarking on a voyage of discovery that leads to the immeasurable beauty that lies within you. Each morning when you awake, you are provided with a gourmet breakfast for the spirit and soul with the hidden manna of your dreams.

Recommended Books

A Course in Miracles, published by the Foundation for Inner Peace, Tiburon, CA 1975. The Text, Workbook & Manual remind you that you are perfect and that you are Love when you allow yourself to see with spiritual vision. It teaches you how to change your thought pattern from one of fear, lack, attack and blame through forgiveness (release that it was never "real" in the first place) to acceptance of love; looking beyond what you perceive to the truth of all things. In this lies true peace.

How I Used Truth by H. Emilie Cady. Unity School Christianity Publisher, 1950. Lee's Summit, Mo. This book deals with how to apply the principles of Truth to our lives and how to prove it for ourselves.

Law of Life, Vol.,1 & 2 by A.D. Luk, A.D. Luk Publications, CO. 1960. These volumes give an understanding of fundamental truths, universal law and principles, with practical application. They help us to accept our own God Presence and to trust our I AM PRESENCE.

Love is Letting Go of Fear by Gerald G. Jampolsky, M.D. Bantam Books, NY. 1979. This will help you to realize that you have a choice in selecting peace or conflict for yourself. A Course in Miracles is the source of the lessons contained in it. A national bestseller of his is "Goodbye to Guilt".

Pray and Grow Rich by Catherine Ponder, Parker Publishing Co. 1968. She has many books including *The Dynamic Laws of Prosperity*, *The Dynamic Laws of Healing*, *Prosperity Secrets of the Ages*. Her books are Christian oriented and metaphysical in nature.

The Impersonal Life by Joseph S. Benner, DeVorss & Co., 1941. This text helps to make clear the way out of all your problems. It explains the wisdom and strength that show you how to bring peace, health and the abundance of all your heart's desires. We are taught to

BE STILL and KNOW THAT I AM GOD. It is telling your ego that you are one with GOD and not ruled by ego. Another book by Benner is called THE WAY TO THE KINGDOM.

The Only Diet There Is by Sondra Ray, Celestial Arts, 1981. "It's about going all the way, looking at your problems, the reason for them, the surrendering of them to the Holy Spirit and releasing yourself totally. To love yourself and those around you." Sondra Ray also has other books, one is a Summary to A Course in Miracles. It beautifully summarizes the Course and has practical applications as well for you.

The Twelve Powers of Man by Charles Fillmore. Unity School of Christianity Publishers, Unity Village, MO. This book deals "with forces that function below and above the field of the conscious mind, the subconscious mind and the superconscious mind."

Super Beings by John Randolph Price. Quartus Foundation, 1981. Austin, TX. He "invites you to move up to the level of mastery." It's a "How to" book...how to be well spiritually, mentally, emotionally, physically, and financially so you will be ready in consciousness to take your place in the new world of the Superbeings." Other books are the Abundance Book (40 Day Prosperity Plan) and a 60 Day non-Human Plan and many others.

The Power of Your Subconscious Mind by Dr. Joseph Murphy, Prentice-Hall, 1963. Discover the nature of your subconscious and use it to create the highest and best reality.

As a Man Thinketh by James Allen, Putnam Publishing Group. The original 1902 classic is available in many formats.

Super Vita-Minds: How to Stop Saying I Hate You...To Yourself. Padaran Publications 1997. This is a book on how to feed the subconscious mind with super love thoughts that erase the race consciousness thought patterns, with the guidance of the Holy Spirit. Co-author Daya Devi-Doolin's other books are mentioned at the beginning of this book.

www.ingramcontent.com/pod-product-compliance
Lightning Source LLC
Chambersburg PA
CBHW070647050426
42451CB00008B/300